THE TRAP:

THE MAKING OF THE SENIOR PASTOR OF THE TRAP

(Based On a True Story)

Dr. Larry Powell

Praise For the Making of The Senior Pastor of the TRAP

"Superman, He-Man, the Incredible Hulk, Samson, names we associate with great strength. But make sure to add Dr. Larry Powell to that list. From the streets to the church house, I've watched him face every mental, physical, and spiritual battle and still stand ten toes down, head high, praising the Lord. A true definition of strength and a real man of God."

~ *Gerry Pullens, Recruiting Coordinator, 4:13 Strong*

"Every part of this man's life has been shattered into pieces from the dangers of street life and time in prison to the unimaginable loss of his children. Yet God had a master plan from the very beginning to mold him into a vessel fit for His use and a reflection of His glory. Truly, a story of Amazing Grace."

~ *Frank Turner Jr., Pastor, Author, and Friend*

"Larry's story stands apart it speaks to those we hope to deter from incarceration and inspires those ready to rise and make a difference. He has lived it, survived it, and now shares it. His powerful testimony of redemption and resilience is one the world needs to hear."

~ *Ruby Joyner, Chief of Corrections*

"When I think about who Larry truly is, five qualities rise to the surface, each one proven, not claimed: Loyal. Determined. Strong. Obedient. Godly. Larry showed me what it really means to have a true accountability partner. His loyalty isn't something he talks about; it's something he lives. With him, what you see is what you get: authenticity, strength, and a steady presence that doesn't change with the seasons. Now, through *The Trap,* the world gets to witness what we've seen for years: a man who didn't just escape the trap, he transformed it."

~ *Darryl Moore (D. Moe), Brother in Christ*

Praise For the Making of The Senior Pastor of the TRAP

"The hard work and passion Larry poured into this book are evident on every page. His commitment to telling his truth with honesty and courage makes his journey impossible to ignore. Writing a book requires real determination, and he has demonstrated that and more. *The Trap* is more than a story; it's a testimony of resilience, purpose, and transformation. This book is positioned to impact countless lives."

~ *Zay Maxwell, Founder of Still Standing Foundation, Loyal Friend*

THE TRAP: THE MAKING OF THE SENIOR PASTOR OF THE TRAP

Published by BN Publications LLC
P.O. Box 60194
Nashville, TN 37206
Names: Powell, Larry, Author. 1977
Editor: Pamela Cosby
Pg. 44 Exhibit (A) –Dr. Larry Powell
Title: The Trap: The Making of The Senior Pastor of the Trap
Description: First Edition.
Includes bibliographical references and author reflections.
Identifiers:
ISBN 979-8-218-83926-0 (paperback)

Subjects:
LCSH: Christian life Conversion. | Faith and Transformation. |
Street ministry | African American clergy Biography

Printed in the United States of America

1 2 3 4 5 6 7 8 9 10

Book Cover Design by Dr. Larry Powell

This book is the true story of how I grew from a drug dealer to a Senior Pastor of The Trap, from the streets to the sanctuary. *The Trap* is more than a title; it's the bridge between who I was and who God called me to be.

For many, the word "trap" means a place, a block, a corner, or a house where drug deals go down and survival is the goal. But for me, *the trap* became something deeper. It represented a mindset, a cycle, a struggle. It was the weight of poverty, violence, addiction, and the pain of losing people I loved.

What you'll read in these pages isn't just a story, it's a testimony of transformation. The trap that once tried to take my life became the very tool God used to change it. This is not just a title; it's a legacy-one built through faith, endurance, and the kind of resilience only God can produce.

– *Dr. Larry Powell*

MENTEE

FOREWORD

When I first met Larry, he wasn't "Pastor," like I call him now, or "Dr. Powell." Back then, he was just Larry, the man everyone in the streets knew and respected. Back then, we were both in the trap, chasing money, trying to survive, and running from pain we didn't yet know how to name. I was younger, looking up to him because of his reputation and presence. He was the kind of man the streets talked about, not for what he said, but for what he stood for. What I didn't know then was that I was standing next to a man God was already shaping for something far greater.

When Larry gave his life to Christ, it wasn't just talk; it was a transformation. I saw it with my own eyes. I watched a man walk away from the game, from the same streets that built him, and step into a calling that changed everything. He didn't just find religion; he found purpose.

Before meeting him, I honestly believed people like us didn't get second chances. The streets convince you that once you're in, you're marked forever either by a number, a name, or a grave. But Larry showed me something different. He showed me that God can meet you right where you are in the pain, in the chaos, in the trap and still pull you into purpose. He made faith feel real for somebody like me, somebody from the hood.

What makes Larry different as a mentor is how genuine he is. He doesn't preach from a pedestal he walks with you through your process. He listens before he lectures. He doesn't try to make you feel small for what you've done; he reminds you of what God can still do. He lives his testimony out loud, not to show off, but to show that change is possible.

For me, *The Trap* isn't just a book title, it's a reflection of life itself. It represents the valley I had to go through to start my own journey. There's pain in that valley, but there's purpose in it too. I'm still learning, still growing, still trying to apply what he's taught me. Larry's story reminds me that it truly does "get greater later" when you surrender fully to God.

His journey proves that no matter how far you've fallen, there's still room to rise. Watching him climb from the streets to the stage, from prison to the pulpit keeps me grounded in faith. Every time I see him speak, I'm reminded that what God starts, He finishes. If I had to describe Larry in three words, I'd say he's honest, resilient, and faithful. Honest enough to face his past, resilient enough to rise above it, and faithful enough to never forget where he came from.

Dr. Larry Powell is living proof that redemption is real. His story reminds us all that no matter the mistakes, no matter the time lost, God can still rewrite the ending.

-Sylvester Mosley aka Slick, Mentee, and Brother in Christ

MENTOR

FOREWORD

Dr. Joseph W. Walker, III
Mount Zion Baptist Nashville

There are stories that offer information, and then there are stories that offer impartation, narratives that not only document a journey but deposit something into the soul of the reader. The life of Dr. Larry Powell is such a story. As his pastor and mentor, I have had the privilege of walking alongside him through some of life's most complex and challenging seasons. I have witnessed the weight of loss, the sting of disappointment, and the pressure of adversity attempt to suffocate his progress. And yet, in every difficult moment, I have also witnessed a resilience that can only be produced by the hand of God. His journey echoes the words of the Apostle Paul, "We are hard pressed on every side, yet not crushed; perplexed, but not in despair" (2 Corinthians 4:8).

What you hold in your hands is far more than a memoir; it is a modern-day parable of redemption. In academic discourse, Howard Thurman wrote about the "inward sea," the interior life shaped and reshaped by divine encounter. Dr. Powell's story is evidence of this spiritual formation proof that God does His greatest work not in the absence of struggle but in the midst of it. His transformation illustrates what Dietrich Bonhoeffer once argued: that grace is never cheap; it is costly, but it is also powerful enough to reclaim, reorder, and repurpose a life.

From the trap house to the Lord's house, his life embodies Joseph's proclamation in Genesis 50:20: "What the enemy meant for evil, God meant for good." Through discipline, humility, and unwavering faith, Dr. Powell has become a living testament to the redemptive capacity of God. I have seen him grow spiritually, intellectually, and emotionally into a leader who now stands boldly in the very places where brokenness once tried to bury him.

This book is not simply worth reading, it is essential. It speaks to anyone who has ever wondered if God can use their past, redeem their pain, or write purpose from chaos. As you engage these pages, expect to encounter a testimony that will challenge your thinking, strengthen your faith, and remind you that destiny is undefeated. God is still raising up voices from unlikely places, and Dr. Larry Powell is one of them.

- Dr. Joseph W. Walker, III

TABLE OF CONTENTS

Chapter 1:
"The Early Trap"

Smile on me, your servant; teach me the right way to live.
Psalm 119:135

Playing illegal numbers for my folks was my first introduction to the hustle. By the time I was eleven, my mind was already in the dope game, even though I had never touched it. I hadn't sold anything, never stood on the block for real, but the streets already whispered my name.

Pops: "Aye, boy! Get that number book and write this down."

He called out numbers like they were Scripture:

"713 two dollars straight. 504 three-dollar box."

I grabbed the number book and wrote as neatly as I could. This wasn't schoolwork. This was hustling a different kind of math.

Pops: "Take this number ticket and twenty-five dollars to Spoonie. Don't use Main Street. Hit the alley and don't stop and talk to anybody."

Those numbers weren't just digits. They were dreams, a poor man's prayer wrapped in risk. More often than not, those numbers brought food to the table and clothes for our backs. Before the State of Tennessee ever thought about a lottery, this was ours.

Unlike most kids in my neighborhood, my chores weren't taking out the trash or mowing the lawn. My father played the numbers, so he sent me to deliver his picks. The first time, I was nervous, unsure of what to expect. But Spoonie, the number man, didn't care. He barely looked at me, probably because Pops had been his customer for years. From then on, delivering numbers became my daily task. It was interesting, sure, but it got in the way of what I wanted most to play ball and hang with my friends.

My father, Larry Thomas Powell everybody called him Larry was always hustling. Tall, dark-skinned, handsome, he carried himself with that pretty-boy swagger. He made ends meet however he could: playing numbers, fixing cars as a shade-tree mechanic, doing plumbing on the side. His steady gig was at Goodyear as a professional tire technician, but eventually he opened his own place Larry's Tire Shop on Dickerson Road.

My mother, Dorothy Mae Hayes, worked as a unit clerk at Bordeaux Hospital. She was wise, responsible, and loved my father fiercely maybe too much. Sometimes I felt she could've done better for herself, but she stayed committed to her marriage. Together they raised me and, four years later, my little brother Eric, whom we called E for short. E favored my father; he grew to be about 5'10. Folks in the family called me Pumpkin since I was a baby. Growing up, it stuck. Some just called me P. Very few people knew me as Larry.

Running numbers was serious business. Players picked three digits, hoping to hit on 000 to 999. Illegal, risky, but for Pops, it was survival. For me, it became a responsibility, a responsibility I couldn't avoid, but I learned to accept the path. My route to Spoonie's trailer was through the alley behind our backyard. The path was worn from neighbors cutting through. I'd crunch across broken bottles and step over crack pipes, keeping my eyes forward. I knew these were things a kid shouldn't see. Sometimes people lounged in backyards, watching me. They knew exactly where I was headed; most of them had walked that same path themselves, chasing the hope that this time, these numbers might finally be the ones.

Spoonie had a trailer next to the corner store. I'd push the creaky door open and step inside, the smell of smoke and old paper hanging in the air. Behind a worn desk sat Spoonie, calm and steady, like he'd been doing this forever. There wasn't much conversation beyond a quick nod or greeting. No small talk, no questions asked. I'd slide the tickets across the desk, he'd take them without a word, and just like that, my part was done. I'd turn and head back home, my sneakers crunching across the gravel outside, already thinking about what I was missing out on with my friends.

By evening, we'd all be glued to Channel 20, the station out of Chicago. The lottery was legal there, and it was also the same channel we watched Bulls basketball games on. Every night, families across the neighborhood gathered around their TVs, waiting for the winning numbers. That's how the community found out together, including Spoonie and the other number runners who had picked up tickets that day. Some nights, the numbers brought joy, like a sudden blessing dropped out of the sky. Other nights, they brought nothing but disappointment. But no matter the outcome, there was always hope, and that hope kept people coming back.

I didn't care much for school. What kept me going were the few things I enjoyed: math, gym, lunch, and later, workshop classes. Everything else felt like a blur; I just had to get through. After the last bell rang, I'd watch men roll through the neighborhood in flashy cars, the kind with polished rims that glinted in the sun. They wore clothes I'd never seen before, nothing like Pops' work uniforms or Mom's hospital scrubs. Their world looked bigger, brighter, and unreachable. And I couldn't help but be drawn to it. They lived on another level; one I secretly wanted to reach.

Our home at 1021 Jackson Street sat in the middle of North Nashville, 37208 (later became the highest incarceration zip code in the world). It was lively, intense, and complicated, a real hood community. Neighbors like Miss Billie kept the block close-knit. Her family would throw cookouts that lasted all night. Kids played kickball in the street until 2 a.m., and every Sunday, her daughter Kim took all of us to the Rivergate Skate Center. Despite the vice and violence, we felt safe and connected. But even while playing with others as a kid, I knew I had already seen too many deaths in and around my community for a kid my age.

Summers meant piling into the car and heading to Mississippi, Bolivar County, Merigold. That's where my roots were, with grandparents, great-grandparents, and cousins too many to count. I spent time with my great-grandfather on Dad's side, John Gordon, and my grandfather on Mom's side, Frank Hayes. Family and tradition ran deep.

It's probably safe to say that the choices made by the men in my family and the environment of the neighborhood I grew up in shaped the way I would live my life, the paths I would take. As a kid in North Nashville, my so-called "entertainment" wasn't cartoons or video games; it was watching the Metro Vice Squad roll into our neighborhood like clockwork. On Tuesdays and Thursdays, they'd set up shop on the corner of 10th and Jackson, parking under a nearby tree that everybody on the block knew. I learned their routine quick. Two RVs and about seven unmarked police cars would flood the street, while three undercover officers dressed like any other dude in the hood were already in place, selling $10 and $20 bags of weed. Back then, weed came in little gold bags, not sandwich bags like later. After making a sale, the undercover would call it in, and an unmarked car would swoop in to pull the buyer over, slap on the cuffs, and haul him off. And once Metro Vice packed up and left, the real hustlers came out to make their money, business as usual.

My friend Mike was one of those hustlers. I remember him standing under that same tree, trying to scrape together some money selling weed. He wanted me to join him in the game; he thought I had what it took. But at the time, I was still trying to be a good kid, trying to hold onto what little innocence I had left. Mike had moved with his parents from the West side to the North, but he never really left his old life behind. He spent his time running back and forth between both sides of town, hustling, pushing weed wherever he could. Years later, the game caught up to him. He was gunned down by another black man, his hustle cut short in the same streets that raised us both.

In 1989, when I was about twelve, my family moved from Jackson Street to 24th Avenue North, and I started going to DuPont Tyler Middle School. Life in the new neighborhood had its own rhythm. On my daily trip to the number house, I met a lot of guys who were into way more than just playing numbers. We would play football or basketball in the neighborhood field. I'd be mid-drill or about to score, and then here came my little brother, E, calling me off the court. Pops had sent him to remind me I had a number run to make. E thought it was the funniest thing in the world, watching me drop the ball and head off to Spoonie's. It was his way of getting back at me for not letting him tag along with me and my friends. What annoyed me only entertained him.

I admired the drug dealers' cars more than I should have. David, a guy in our neighborhood, had two of the best-looking Cadillac Sevilles I'd ever laid eyes on. The two-tone paint job glistened in the sun, and the car moved like it was alive, powered by two hydraulic switches. The short front end and rims gave it an edge, like it was made to be noticed. David had the same kind of swagger, mean, confident, and sharp. He wore MCM jogging suits, thick gold ropes, and his name carried weight at Club G's, the hottest spot in the city back then. To me, David was living the dream. I'd picture myself sliding behind the wheel of a Seville, pulling up to G's, and stepping inside like I owned the night. But that was just my imagination. David would disappear from my story; he was not a part of the dream that awaited me.

I was good friends with Robert Brooks; we met in school and clicked right away. We went to basketball games together, played video games, and kicked it after class like most kids our age. But after a few months, I started to notice things changing. Robert's school attendance dropped lower and lower. At first, I'd look for him in the usual spots where we hung out, but he was never there. Weeks passed without seeing him, and then weeks stretched into months.

When I finally did see Robert again, he didn't look like the same kid I knew. He carried himself differently, flashing gold ropes and wearing MCM jogging suits, looking more like David the hustler everybody in the neighborhood knew than a classmate. I found out Robert had been running with a big-time hustler "Lil Clyde", from the West side, and I couldn't shake the thought: *"Robert got on too fast. This can't be weed money."*

Before I ever got the chance to talk to him about it, tragedy hit. His own girlfriend killed him. To this day, I still don't know why.

Even then, I wanted to know what it felt like to slide behind the wheel of one of those drug dealers' cars, to drape heavy gold chains across my neck, to walk around in clothes that turned heads. I could see as clear as day that living like that meant making money in a different way. A fast-food job or the kind of part-time work most kids my age did would never bring in the kind of cash needed for that lifestyle. And I knew it would take more than selling weed to stack money that fast. That's when I met Joe Buster, who quickly became a good friend. Joe Buster was sharp, street smart, but he also loved basketball and football, just like me. One afternoon, while we were talking, Joe Buster brought up a name I'd been hearing around the neighborhood: Lil' Pete. He asked if I knew him. The name was familiar because everybody spoke of Lil' Pete like he was larger than life, almost like he was God. His sister lived nearby, so I'd see him whenever he came around to visit her.

I officially met Lil' Pete at the number house. He carried himself in a way that made people stop and notice. Laid back but always flashy. His bald head was always clean and shining, his clothes were stylish, and he never pulled up in anything less than a nice car. He knew the dope game inside and out. I had no business being at the number house at all, but Pops kept sending me, so I saw him often. If you grew up in 37208, Lil' Pete was your neighborhood superstar. Everybody wanted to be like him. More than a hustler, he was known for looking out for his people, helping families pay bills, buying groceries, and not just around the holidays. His generosity made him more than respected; it made him loved.

To us, before Nashville was ever called Cashville or the IT City, it was known as Lil' Pete City. His name carried the weight of a high and the glitter of material blessings. His reputation didn't stop at 37208; it echoed all the way into Bellevue among the white kids, too. I'll never forget the day I heard one of my white teachers talking about Lil' Pete at school. That's when I realized his name had grown bigger than Nashville itself.

The first time I ever saw a Ferrari in real life; it wasn't on TV or in a magazine; it was when Lil' Pete pulled up to the number house in one. Now, when I think back, it was an 'Acura that mirrored a Ferrari. He was also the first Black man I ever saw behind the wheel of a seven-seat Land Cruiser.

Joe Buster spotted him in that same Land Cruiser at the Kentucky Derby, and the Kentucky boys couldn't get enough of him. His success in the dope game made people gravitate toward him. The way he put Nashville on the map was unbelievable. He even once bought a bulletproof Benz from Shaquille O'Neal at the Freak Nic in Atlanta.

In 1989, Lil' Pete took an '89 Chevy Blazer, put a Ferrari kit on it, chopped the top, painted it royal blue, and threw on some rims called hammers. Years later, in 2002, women were still drawn to take pictures with the Chevy Blazer. That's how clean it stayed. Lil' Pete wasn't just flashy for himself. He bought kids Jordans for school, paid gas and electric bills for struggling families he looked out for in his neighborhood in ways most hustlers didn't, he was major. You know that Lexus Coupe on the cover of Kool Daddy Fresh's "It's All True" CD cover, that was Lil Pete's.

Lil Pete's Story

Lil Pete was like a legend to the streets. Everybody knew him, and when he was killed, it sent a shockwave through the city. His death wasn't just another headline; it hurt the whole community. He didn't deserve to go out like that, but the truth of the game is cold: if you don't surrender, the only exits are death or jail.

On February 21, 1997, near TSU, that broken bridge grew darker. Rabbit pulled a gun on Lil Pete, robbed him, and left him dead over some bricks of cocaine. That year, Rabbit went on a killing spree, leaving scars across the city. And to this day, I still wonder what made Lil Pete trust him in the first place.

I'll never forget his funeral. No church in the city would host it not because Pete didn't deserve a service, but because they were afraid. Afraid of the crowd it would bring, afraid of the image it carried. That moment showed me something bigger: the church had lost its influence over us.

Our reality, the dope, the violence, the hustling, the broken families, wasn't welcomed in the church. They didn't know how to handle us, didn't know how to sit down with young men who lived and breathed survival. Instead of pulling us closer, they pulled away. They wanted order, structure, control. But our lives were chaos, and we needed someone who could step into that chaos and understand the struggle, not just preach against it.

When the church stepped back, it left a hole. And in that void, we clung to voices like 2Pac voices that didn't shy away from our pain, but spoke it out loud, raw and unfiltered. After Lil Pete's death, the streets were hurting. That's when 2Pac's voice meant the most. Pac wasn't just a rapper; he was the soundtrack to our pain and survival. He spoke directly to the D-boys in a way the church couldn't, because the church didn't understand us. While they turned their backs, Pac leaned in.

Through his music, he acknowledged the struggle the poverty, the betrayal, the nights of hustling just to see another sunrise. He didn't sugarcoat it or preach down at us. He rapped about living with contradictions: praying but still carrying heat, wanting better but still drowning in the streets. For young Black men who felt trapped between hope and destruction, Pac gave language to our reality. He couldn't save us, but he helped heal wounds the church never touched. His words stitched together some of the broken pieces in us that Sunday mornings ignored. Pac was proof that even in the dirt, somebody still saw our humanity.

But while the streets celebrated him, my mom and the D.A.R.E. program at Buena Vista Middle drilled a different message into me: *Never, ever do drugs or sell drugs.* Anytime the news ran a story about a drug bust, or we heard about someone we knew getting caught, my mom would launch into her speech, "Don't you ever-ever-ever do or sell drugs." She meant every word. I'd hear her talking to her sister Joyce on the phone, her voice rising as she described how crack was tearing apart families in Mound Bayou, Mississippi. One hustler, she said, had been hauling crack all the way from Texas. She made sure we were listening. She didn't have to say much, because by then the crack epidemic had already taken hold, spreading from the inner cities into small towns and rural communities all over the country. It wasn't just a neighborhood problem; it was a national crisis.

I remember when President George H. W. Bush went on national television in 1989, sitting in the Oval Office, and held up a small bag of crack cocaine that had been seized just across the street from the White House. He called it the nation's number one enemy and declared a full-out "War on Drugs." But no matter what was said on TV, in neighborhoods like mine, the crack kept coming. Families were torn apart, communities collapsed, and prisons started filling faster than ever. For us, it wasn't just politics or headlines it was everyday life.

Later that year, my grandfather on my mom's side passed, and we went to Mississippi for his funeral. While there, I was with my uncle Ricky when we stopped by a friend's house, Martin Harris. Martin sat at his kitchen table, breaking down little white rocks from one big white rock. That was the first time I saw crack with my own eyes. Martin slid a few rocks to my uncle, and we left. It came out later that my uncle was climbing in the game fast, and the only person in the family who knew was me.

Meanwhile, back in Cashville, crews like the Bottom Boyz in East Nashville and the Delk Boys in the North were blowing up, just like my uncle down South. These weren't grown men, they were kids my age driving Cadillacs. One of the Bottom Boyz even hit the city with the first Lexus Drop Head years before the dealership ever sold luxury convertibles. That car was worth $65,000.

In my own neighborhood, there was a guy we called Dirty Black. He was funny, slick with card tricks, everybody knew he was sharp. "One weekend, he disappeared. A month later, we found out he'd been locked up, strung out on drugs.

When he came home, you knew it. Every Saturday, a system blasted from an old-school car at his mama's house. Soon after, I saw him driving a Cadillac Seville with gold bones. At first, I thought maybe he'd hit the numbers. But when that car sat parked for weeks, I knew better. Next, he showed up in a two-door Benz, then a customized drop-top black Chevy truck, and later another Seville, all laced in gold. That's the thing about the streets: you could be broke one day and counting stacks the next. Dirty Black got on fast, but not with crack. He was moving K4s Dilaudids, beans, out East, and the money was coming in faster than any crack money. First person I saw prevail in the pill game.

By this time, the crack itself was sweeping through Nashville like an F4 tornado, leaving families torn apart and neighborhoods gutted. Nobody was safe. People were smoking it through TVs, radios, and car antennas, anything they could turn into a pipe. That's when the word "crackhead" hit the streets. Still, crack gave young black kids from poor family's access to thousands, sometimes millions. Thirteen- and fourteen-year-olds were flipping $200 worth of crack into $400, doubling it again and again, hiding $24,000 or more in houses, shoeboxes, or stashed anywhere they could. Out East, K4s hit with the same force, and the money was just as fast. But fast money brought even faster pain. With so many tears came an ocean of grief that drowned families all over the city.

By now, I knew what it would take to live the way I wanted to, ride in those cars, wear those clothes, and step into that life. I was fifteen, had my driver's permit, and I was getting closer to it every day. Between getting a haircut at Tiffany's Car Wash, dropping off Pops' number tickets at Spoonie's, and hanging out on Delk watching guys race to cars to catch a sale, I had already seen enough to know what the streets demanded. As much as I hated running numbers for Pops, I didn't have a choice. If I didn't, I'd catch hell when I got home, especially if Pops had sent E to find me and made sure I was back, doing the work he wanted me to do. I'd overhear my mom pleading with him to stop making me do his dirty work, but it never changed anything. "The only time the pace eased up was when Spoonie started coming by the house himself to pick up the tickets. With him handling the pickups, a weight lifted off me, my load felt lighter, and the grind wasn't as heavy."

Chapter 2:
Surviving the Wicked East Trap

Don't let the errors of evil people lead you down
the wrong path and make you lose your balance.
2 Peter 3:17

In 1991, my family packed up and moved to what I would come to call The Wicked East. Our new home sat on West Eastland Avenue, a stretch that ran from Gallatin Road to North 9th Street and McFerrin Avenue. I didn't want to leave the North side of Nashville. I cried like a baby the day we moved. The only thing that eased the pain was knowing my parents would still let me go to school out North.

That very first night in East Nashville, I looked out our living room window and witnessed something I'll never forget. The Chicamauga Boys were beating a crackhead senseless in the street. Their name came from the block most of them lived on, Chicamauga, between Seymour and West Eastland. What they probably didn't know was that their street was named after the Battle of Chickamauga in 1863, where Confederate soldiers secured Nashville as a supply base for the North.

Just like their name, the Chicamauga Boys lived by a battle reputation. They were known for whipping people, no questions asked. So, when younger hustlers from West Eastland tried to stand up to them in the dope game, it took real guts. At first, I hated the East Side. But it didn't take long before I started to love it, once I saw how the streets here worked differently. Pops had even found his own lane. He got a plug on weed out of Texas and opened a tire shop on Dickerson Road, mixing hustle with entrepreneurship in his own way.

I loved it when Pops left the house to sell his weed. That was the only time there was real peace at home. Before heading out, he'd take a long bath, splash on some good-smelling cologne, and light up a joint. The scent of smoke mixed with the cologne hung in the air, strangely comforting to me.

Now, Pops was either careless or he trusted us too much, because he'd leave bags of money and pounds of weed lying around his bedroom like it was nothing. Sometimes it would sit there for weeks before he even touched it. One day, I couldn't resist anymore, I helped myself to a little money and a little weed.

When it came to his kids, Pops had a strange philosophy. He hated when Mom bought us nice clothes and didn't believe in keeping us in the latest fashion. To this day, I don't know why. Once, he surprised me with a winter coat. But instead of something I could wear proudly, it had three pink rings around the sleeve and a pink ski man stitched across the back. Back then, pink was considered a girl's color, and I couldn't understand why my father wanted me to wear it. Most likely, he picked it up cheap off somebody in the streets.

When I wore it to school, I paid the price. Big Johnny, the class clown, rolled into one and went in on me all day. His jokes hit like punches. Still, I held my ground and fired back, because if you didn't, Johnny would roast you until you broke. I'd seen other kids leave his burn sessions in tears, but I refused to give him that satisfaction.

Growing up, I disliked my dad. I always wished Mom would leave him, but she never did. By the time I was old enough to drive, I'd already started selling weed for myself. I finally had a little independence with my license and my own car. But just when I thought I was free, Pops pulled me right back into his hustle. He started making me run numbers to the North side again.

E was going to school out East and spent most of his time on that side of town, so at least I didn't have to worry about him chasing me down for Pops. Still, Pops kept me on a leash. If I didn't get home in time to turn in his tickets, he'd threaten to take my car away. I lost my license once, but that didn't stop him. I still had to make the runs, risking trouble with the police and making things even worse for myself.

Eventually, Pops found a number house in East Nashville that he liked. The bad news? I was still the one stuck turning in his tickets. The number house was a magnet for dope boys nobody else hung around there. Around 1997, I started noticing changes in E. He stopped eating at home, which was strange even for a fourteen-year-old. He'd bring new clothes in and stash them away. I caught him hiding Tommy Hilfiger and Pelle Pelle jackets, along with one of those giant minute phones, making sure Mom and Pops never saw them.

About a year later, tensions in the house finally boiled over. E and I got into a heated argument with Pops, and in the middle of it, he struck Mom. That was all it took. Instinct kicked in, and both E and I jumped in on Pops, putting our hands on him, something I regret to this day.

After that fight, I couldn't stay in the house anymore. I moved in with my Uncle Floyd, who took me in and treated me like his own son. E stayed behind, though, and the atmosphere between him and Pops grew darker. Pops made it clear where the line was drawn. He told E that if he didn't know who Marvin Gaye was and the story of how Marvin had been killed by his own father, he'd better do his homework and learn quickly. The message was clear: follow my rules or pay the price.

Not long after I shared the Marvin Gaye story with him, E went out and bought a stolen .380 pistol off the streets. He said it was for protection from Pops.

Out East, E had fallen in with a new crew who called themselves W.E., short for West Eastland. At the time, some older hustlers already controlled a well-known drug block over on Chicamauga Avenue, and they weren't happy about these younger W.E. boys setting up shop in the alley that separated the two streets. Before long, a drug war broke out that stretched on for months. Every other day it seemed like there was another fight.

Somehow, no one got killed during that stretch, though it came close more than once. Big David, a dealer from our block, got into it with a dude named Ty. Their beef escalated until one day Ty shoved him straight through a window. A shard of glass stabbed Big David in the stomach, coming dangerously close to a main artery. By some miracle, he survived.

Watching all of this unfold, I realized just how deep my little brother was getting with these men. I had no idea the kind of world he was entangled in until I saw it with my own eyes.

Three months later, Metro P.D. pulled up out of nowhere and started searching everybody hanging out on the block. E and I had been out there, just kicking it with some folks from the street. What happened next is something I'll never forget.

One of the officers slipped on plastic gloves, stepped up to E, and reached straight down his pants. He pulled out an 8-ball of crack cocaine from E's butt crack and shouted loud enough for everyone to hear:

"We got booty dope, guys!"

I couldn't believe what I was seeing. Later, I found out E had another 8-ball stashed under his testicles. We hid crack in some of the wildest places but seeing that moment unfold explained a lot about the way E had been acting over the past year.

Even though I wasn't living at Pops' house anymore, I'd come by sometimes to check on E and chill in his room. He was always on edge around me. That's when I noticed he had a combination lock on his closet. He guarded that closet with his life never opening it when I was there. To this day, I don't know how Pops never caught on, but somehow E always managed to stay on his good side.

Before they hauled him off, E slipped me the combination and told me to "come get him." At the time, I didn't understand what he meant, but later I opened that closet. Inside were shoeboxes stacked with cash. I stopped counting at twenty thousand dollars. My first thought was, *Dang, Lil' Bro you really balling.*

I couldn't believe he had that much money tucked away. Part of me wondered if he was hitting up Pops the same way I had, but then I thought, *why crack?* He knew how much mom preached against dope. Still, there it was E living a whole double life right under Pops' nose.

That night, Mom picked him up from juvenile detention. I kept thinking about the closet, the money, and all the things I didn't know about my little brother. Pops was still leaving pounds of weed and bags of money all over his bedroom without saying a word, and I couldn't figure out if E had found his own lane or if he was dipping into Pops' stash like me. Either way, he had stopped coming out North completely, so I decided to find out what had him so tied up in the East.

The truth was, E had skills that could have taken him down a totally different road. He was gifted as a barber, able to cut Black or white hair with the same precision. He could've been one of Nashville's top barbers if he'd pursued it. But the streets had called him louder than the clippers, and he answered.

Not long after the Big David situation, I started getting introduced around as E's brother. That's when it hit me, he had been out there long enough to build a name for himself. The W.E. boys had gone so hard against the Chicamauga crew that eventually even they backed off, saying, *"It's enough money out here for everybody."*

By then, I was spending more and more time on West Eastland myself. The money was unreal. A customer might spend forty dollars, leave, and come back thirty minutes later with another forty. Some of them would just burn through all their cash in one day. I watched E take a quarter ounce of crack worth two hundred dollars and flip it into over seven hundred without breaking a sweat. Compared to that, weed money was slow.

One day I took E back out North to buy from Homeboy, a dude I'd known for years. Homeboy had been in and out of juvenile and prison his whole life, but prison never changed him. To him, it was just a resting place, somewhere to regroup before getting back in the game.

E only wanted an ounce, but I kept telling him to buy more. *"Get half a bird or a whole bird,"* I'd say. *"Run it up when you get back out East."* The logic was simple: the more you buy, the more you make. But E always played it cautiously. He bought three ounces when I knew he had bird money.

Back out East, we'd run into Ray, a crackhead known for cooking up that thunder crack. E would sell out quickly and be right back looking for Homeboy again. I told him more than once, *"Don't buy less than a four and a baby. Buy bigger, save time, make more money."* But he stuck to two ounces, maybe three at a time. I couldn't figure out why he played small when the chance to level up was right there in his hands.

Chapter 3:
Aimless Living in the Trap

If people can't see what God is doing, they stumble all over themselves;
but when they attend to what he reveals, they are most blessed.
Proverbs 29:18

Coming out of East Nashville, the money was fast, but so was the pain. Watching E dive deeper into the game and seeing the chaos around us left me torn between wanting more and questioning what it was all worth. I had seen the highs, the cars, the clothes, the stacks of cash, but I had also seen how quickly it could all disappear. By the time I stepped into my own hustle, I was carrying not just the lessons of the streets, but also the weight of my own disappointments.

After a few bad decisions and being unhappy with the direction my life was going, I started selling crack. I was down so bad, ashamed and disappointed in myself, that I even contemplated suicide. Trying to deal with it all on my own without asking for help, that's always been one of my biggest struggles. Getting deep into the crack game meant hustling all day, every day, starting with whatever product and money I had in my hand and grinding to turn it into more.

I started with just half a gram. Off that, I made $40. Out of what I earned, I took $5, bought some crackers, lunch meat, and a 50-cent drink from the machine, which left me with $35 for my re-up. That time, I only made my money back, but the next time, I managed to double up.

Before then, I had never even heard of a double up, but Joe Ski always looked out for me. Joe Ski was tall, light-skinned, with braids straight to the back, and for some reason, he always seemed to be around whenever I needed him. With his help, I made $75 off that first double up, only to fall right back off again. Part of me wanted to quit selling dope altogether and go back to just hustling weed while picking up a side job. But the truth was, I had no money, no purpose, and no real direction in life.

E wasn't about that double-up life. He'd rather sell tenth for tenth and stretch it out slow and steady. So I never asked him for help. Instead, I linked with Joe Ski whenever I could. But eventually, even he admitted he was losing too much, and the grind wasn't worth it. Joe Ski was tied in with the West Eastland Empire, and through him, I saw just how deep the hustle really ran.

Around that same time, E told me about three sisters who had just moved from the West side to West Eastland, right next door to our parents. They weren't alone either three of their female cousins were always around. From the moment they showed up, they shifted the energy of the block. These girls stayed lit, smoking weed, barbequing, doing hair, and turning up all night long.

I had never seen women live like that before in the hood. It was like their whole purpose was to keep the party going, and somehow, they did. They brought the project life with them and turned our side of town inside out. Out of that crew came Eboni. She became the mother of my sons Red and J. To me, she was first my baby's mama, later my wife, and eventually my ex-wife. But that's a story I'll unpack later.

When I was at McGavock High School, I got expelled over a fight on the bus. Honestly, I wasn't surprised it happened exactly the way the principal warned me it would. He had told me plain and clear, *"If you fight that boy on the bus, you're out."*

There was a guy named Adam who rode our bus. On most days, he came across as laid back and cool, but one day, he kicked my little brother E in the back. When E came to me crying, I didn't care what the principal had warned me about. My brother needed me. So, I stepped toward Adam, and we fought. Just like the principal said, I was expelled.

I finished out my senior year at Hillwood High. For me, school was never the main thing; it was more like an interruption to my grind. Deep down, I was a good teenager. I wanted a career path and had goals, but the streets kept pulling my focus. Everywhere I looked, there was fast money, and my father's hustle only added fuel to the fire.

I barely got through high school because I was busy selling weed. Most of the time, I was confused about what I really wanted to do with my life. I did graduate, but I don't remember much about those last days, the classes, the teachers, or even graduation itself. School was just something I did to keep mom off my back. What I really wanted was to hurry up, finish, and get my CDL license so I could be ready to drive big trucks by the time I turned twenty-one.

At eighteen, I was the newest hustler on the block. Getting my pack off at first was tough, but I started learning by watching the flow of the other hustlers around me. E, my little brother, was already established just fourteen years old and working the block like it was a full-time job. From 7 a.m. to 7 p.m., he stayed planted, catching everything that came his way. School wasn't a priority for E anymore; the block had become his classroom, and hustling was the only lesson he cared to learn.

There were about seven of us who kept the block covered. Whenever a sell pulled up, somebody in our crew was ready to serve them. My circle included E, Joe Ski, Big David, a dude from Africa we called OD, and Big C. Occasionally, there was a guy named JO. He didn't really have a set routine; he just went with the flow, down for whatever, whenever, however, wherever. Then there was Rah-Rah, a teenager who trailed behind JO like a shadow, doing whatever he did.

The block had one main rule: if your personal sell pulled up, that was automatically yours. Everybody knew who most of the regulars belonged to. Anything else was fair game, and we'd race each other to the cars or whatever vehicle slowed down looking for product. But if your personal sell showed up and you weren't on the block, you were out of luck they got served by whoever spotted them first.

After 7 p.m., E would dip off to handle his own thing. Joe Ski worked whenever he felt like it, sliding in and out. Big David would camp out most of the day, grab whatever he could until third shift, then sit on the block all night. OD stayed on foot, snatching up every sell he saw, but he had one weakness gambling. Anytime a dice game started, you could count on OD getting caught up in it. Rah-Rah, on the other hand, was reckless and moved however he wanted, regardless of the risk. Big C was one of the more experienced hustlers, steady and reliable, the kind of presence that made the block feel balanced. As for me, I didn't smoke, drink, or gamble. That set me apart, but it also gave me an edge. Staying clear-headed made it easier to keep my focus where it needed to be on the hustle.

Even though I stayed committed to the hustle, I always found time for some pleasure. My first flight happened because of a girl. She was a student at Tennessee State University (TSU) that I met at Shoney's breakfast bar, and she lived in Atlanta. Whenever I wanted to see her, I'd hop on a plane, spend a few hours with her, then fly right back. By the time I touched back down in Nashville, I'd be back on the block or at home like I had never even left.

One day, I was rushing back to catch a sell when Officer Ray Barry pulled me over on 3rd Avenue South for speeding, he issued me a speeding ticket and let me go. Fifteen minutes later, I was on the interstate and, believe it or not, the same officer stopped me again this time for jumping lanes on the quick split. That spot was notorious. Drivers coming from out South would always try to cross lanes fast to get back out East. I had done it a hundred times myself and never once thought it was illegal.

But that day, I was rushing to make another sell, and he caught me. I was heated. It felt like the State had made it nearly impossible on purpose, especially since the split sat right in front of the projects. My opinion, it always seemed like another way to trip us up and keep us in the system.

A few weeks later, I found myself back in court for driving on a revoked license. The judge looked me dead in the eye and said, if I ever came back on the same charge, he'd give me a year in jail, day for day.

I tried to reason with him. I asked if I could be approved for a hardship license, something that would at least let me drive to work. He shut that down quickly. That option, he said, was only for DUI offenders. All I could do was shake my head and say, *"Dang."*

At the time, the State wanted almost $10,000 just to reinstate my license. Ten thousand. I couldn't imagine myself doing a year in jail just for driving. The only question was: *Where was I going to get that kind of money?* But deep down, I already knew. If E was pulling bread off the block, I could too. So, I made up my mind I was going to dedicate myself to hustling on the W.E.

When I walked out of court, I had only $25 to my name. I was broken and hungry, so I called Mom and asked if she could bring me some Burger King and let me hold $75. She came through, dropping off a whopper with cheese combo and the cash. Standing there with that food in my hand, I made myself a promise: I was going to grind my way out of this situation, no matter what it took.

There was never a time when a sell pulled up and didn't get served. I treated my business on the block as seriously as a new employee at a high-powered job. While everybody else was gone to the club, I was grinding. When OD went off gambling, I was grinding. When E called it a night, I was grinding. When Joe Ski was out smoking and drinking, I was grinding. Sometimes, I wore the same clothes for days straight. I missed family cookouts, birthdays, and holidays because the block came first.

One day, I pulled up and ran into Shotgun David, one of my regulars. He asked me for a $20 rock, but when he saw the look in my eyes, he stopped and said, *"Never mind. Take this money do whatever you need to do."* He knew that look. He'd seen it in his own reflection after coming home from the penitentiary and hitting the block again.

But a man like Shotgun couldn't go without. He needed that hit. If he didn't get it, something bad was bound to happen either we'd end up killing him for trying to rob us, or he'd hurt one of us trying to take what we had.

I convinced E to give him a wake-up dose, just enough to take the edge off. Shotgun had just come home from serving fifteen years, and you could see it on him. He was cut, strong, and toned from lifting on the yard. Once he got that hit, his head cleared, and he went out to do whatever he had to do to bring money back.

In a way, we were the same. For him, the monkey on his back was crack. For me, it was money. When he got his hit, he could think straight again. And when he handed me that $20, it lifted my monkey at least for a moment until I had to figure out what was next.

Chapter 4:
The Trap Drought of '98

When there's no rain, God still finds a way to make me grow.
Dr Larry Powell

It happens sometimes, and you never see it coming. The suppliers run dry, every source tapped out. A drought could also hit when Metro was swarming the block, making every move too hot to risk. For me, the constant grind of selling has become addictive. The rush of staying busy, of always being on the block, was like fuel and when that slowed down, when the streets went quiet, it threw me off completely.

By Christmas Day 1998, the drought had dragged on, and there was no dope on the streets. That morning, E handed me an 8-ball of butter as a gift. My first thought was, *where did he even get this?* But I didn't ask too many questions. All I knew was that I was now the only one on the block with product. Off that single 8-ball, I pulled in about $400.

But when it was gone, I was right back at zero. E was running low, too. I couldn't waste the profit. I knew it had to go straight into a re-up. Using E's minute phone, I reached out to some people I knew in Memphis. For years, I had heard stories about how heavy they moved and how sharp their game was, and I wanted to see if it was true. This time, I wasn't just chasing a re-up; I was stepping into something bigger.

Memphis didn't fail me; the info checked out. My connection told me to call as soon as I got off the interstate. I didn't want to make the trip alone, so I hyped E up into going with me. He had a license now and bringing him along helped me save every penny. I figured he'd want to grab some work too, and he'd have no problem covering gas and food along the way.

We hit the road around 7 a.m., and by 3 p.m., we were back on the block in Nashville with some of that product they said was the same kind that killed Elvis Presley. That's how strong it was. The drought had gotten so bad that the streets ate it up. Within just a couple of days, I was back at square one, left with only my re-up money to keep going.

Around that time, Eboni Ridley moved from West Eastland to 12th and Buc, one of the city's most well-known drug spots since the '60s. I didn't want her and her sisters to move because they kept our hood alive with their energy. But I knew they loved being close to that element. They brought the same vibe to 12th and Buc, throwing weekly cookouts, dances, and weed parties for their friends and people who lived in the neighborhood. Eboni and I had always flirted with each other, and before long, that turned into something more. Eventually, we hooked up.

I noticed hustlers like Lil' David and his crew whenever I went to hook up with Eboni. David was short, about 5'5", skinny, dark-skinned, and he rocked a platinum grill that lit up his whole mouth. He was cool, but from a distance; you could feel there was more to him than what he showed. Lil' David and his crew had 12th on lock. His name was ringing hard out North, and for a long time, I thought he was the landlord. Out of the six duplexes where Eboni's family lived, Lil' David occupied four of them, each tied to the drug game in some way, including one spot strictly for storage. That meant Eboni and her sisters had no choice but to cross paths with his crew every single day.

Then came the summer of 2000. That's when my life shifted forever. My son, Jawauntez Kendrick Powell, was born, and I became a father at the age of twenty-three. His mother, Eboni, came up with the name, and I was fine with it. I didn't want him to be called Larry.

I'll never forget the moment he entered this world. When the nurse placed him in my arms, it felt as though time had stopped. I couldn't believe my eyes. He was everything I had prayed for in a son. He was my twin. He looked so much like me that even the doctor joked that it looked like I had given birth to him myself. Red, as we later called him, came into the world with a smile on his face. From that very first moment, I knew he was his daddy's baby. At first, we called him Poo. But as he grew, whenever he played outside in the sun, his skin would turn red, and that nickname stuck.

Becoming a father gave me the joy I hadn't felt in years. For a moment, the streets faded into the background. In that hospital room, holding my son, I felt like maybe I had a reason bigger than the block. My role as a new father meant I had to grind even harder. Word on the street was that another hustler, Lil' B, had some work in. As soon as word spread, everybody on the block lined up to place an order with him. My pack was the smallest, but within two hours, I was hitting Lil' B back up.

This time it was different. Because of my new role as a father, I couldn't go back to hitting rock bottom and only having money for re-up. I had a bigger responsibility now, more than just myself. That responsibility made me hungrier, and it made me willing to take bigger risks to keep money in my pocket and provide for my family. So, I moved smarter and faster. I didn't wait until my pack was completely gone before I re-upped. As soon as I made my re-up money, I called Lil' B, and he'd drop off without hesitation. That rhythm kept me coming up. I was stacking about $150 a day. Every time I went to see my baby's mama, I had to pass by Lil' David and his crew. I could feel their eyes on me, and I kept a third eye on them too. Not because I thought they wanted to rob or hurt me, but more like they were asking themselves, *'Why is he hanging over here? What's he trying to start on these streets?"*

In the seven years I'd been grinding and selling work, I had never tried it myself. I was only interested in how it made me money, not how it made me feel. But one day, I got curious and decided to smoke a blunt. It turned out to be a bad decision. Instead of keeping me calm, the weed sent my nerves through the roof. I hated the feeling and told myself I would never touch it again.

Still, that experience left me with something I'll never forget, an awakening I couldn't explain. It took me back to the W.E. days, when I dated a girl from the King's Lane area, whom I would occasionally visit at the Born-Again church. Back then, we called her type of girl's dime pieces; now they'd be called boogie. Our relationship was short-lived, but I remember how being with her gave me a good feeling, like a temporary motivation to do better. But when God made His presence known, it was different. That left me with an awakening I couldn't shake, a weight that pressed deeper than any relationship ever could. Still, even that awakening didn't last long. My mind quickly rerouted back to the streets.

One year, on Super Bowl night, a big house fire broke out across the street from my baby's mama's place. I remember hearing her sister call Los, a guy from the 12th Dog Pound, part of Lil' David's crew. What I figured might happen ended up happening: somebody from my baby's mama's circle had gotten connected with somebody from the 12th Dog Pound.

It turned out the house that caught fire belonged to Lil' David. He was away at the Super Bowl, and I never did find out what caused the fire. But I know this: he took a loss that night. And it could've been worse if Los hadn't kicked in the back door and saved what he could. By this point, the West Eastland section of Nashville had earned its place as one of the city's well-known drug spots.

Business was steady, and Lil' B was still dropping off that straight 8 drop. E decided to buy himself a new Bubble Chevy and enroll in barber school. Me? I had made up my mind I was going to get rich or die trying. To me, this was the only way to make the kind of money I needed to take care of my family and myself.

Even though I didn't live with my baby's mama, I never ran from my responsibilities. I made sure to provide for her and my child. In my mind, if I died trying, so be it would've been worth it. One year, she got a small income tax check and handed me $800 to flip.

Two weeks later, Lil' David caught me outside her house and asked if we could talk.

"Word is you be hustling," he said.

"Yeah," I told him, "I do what I can."

He went on to say he thought the Feds were watching him and he needed to lay low for a while.

"But they're not watching me," I replied. "So, what are you saying?"

He explained that his team wasn't doing right, and he needed a backup move. I wasn't worried about what he had going on. If he needed help moving work, I told him straight up, "Just call me the dump truck."

On my way back out East, Lil' David handed me half an ounce of that drop.

"Take this with you," he said.

"What you want for this?" I asked.

"$350."

I told him I had $350 in my pocket right then, but he shook his head and said, "Pay me when you get it off."

I took it out East, flipped it fast, and brought the money right back. Truthfully, I was hoping he'd let me buy more. Eventually, he did an ounce. Lil' B was charging me $800, while Lil' David only wanted $700. At first, he played me off, but I could tell he was surprised at how quickly I flipped the work and came back with his money.

Three weeks later, word came for me to see him again. This time, he hit me with a four and a split. I paid him off in two days. I was moving the work so fast that Lil' David started pulling from other guys just to keep me supplied. Of course, that caused some friction, but the grind had to be respected.

I never cut Lil' B off completely, but the truth was, I didn't need him anymore. I was paying a lower price, and the quality of the work was just as good. With Lil' David's help, I touched my first $10K. That moment was unforgettable. When I counted that cho, I decided I would never go broke again. I started serving not only the W.E. block but also other hustlers, because I could move anywhere at that point. I was living by the slogan long before NBA YoungBoy ever said it. I refused to let my money fall below $20K (Eight-Four and Half's = 8 CDs of pure cocaine). I was in my federal bag long before MoneyBagg Yo dropped his album.

Being in that bag meant staying on a level where I always had at least $50-65K tucked away, moving with the kind of consistency and discipline that separated real hustlers from the ones just playing at it. I refused to let my money drop below that mark. Every flip, every move I made was about stacking higher, staying sharp, and keeping myself positioned above the small-time hustle.

A young kid started coming around, and I took him under my wing, Lil' Z. I had watched him weigh cocaine like a pro, but when it came to fractions, he struggled. He wanted to sell, but he couldn't break the numbers down. I told him, "If you can weigh cocaine, you can do fractions." I showed him a simple formula, and he caught on quickly. For a while, I thought he would do well, and he did, until he slipped up.

Then Lil' Z went to Mexico on vacation and got caught with over $10K. They locked him up, but he made bond. Instead of facing the case, he escaped and returned to the U.S. The thought of going back to face those charges weighed heavily on him. He knew it was only a matter of time before he'd be sent back, and the idea of spending years in a Mexican prison broke him down. In the end, he committed suicide rather than face that reality. His death hit me hard. He was young, innovative, and had so much ahead of him. But the game doesn't care how much potential you have.

One thing about a drought: having nothing to sell gave us time to step away from the block. We went to Miami, California, and New Orleans to relax and party. My homeboys and I would go to every hood in every city we visited to compare it to ours. And when we were off the clock, we were truly off the clock. It was all about chilling, having fun, and forgetting the grind.

Losing Lil' Z made me feel the urgency of God's call on my life. In 1 Corinthians 16:15, Paul talked about the household of Stephanas being so devoted to their ministry that it became like an addiction they couldn't shake or put down. That scripture hit me because I knew God was calling me similarly. I didn't want to keep seeing people around me trapped in the same cycle, chasing after crack and losing everything to it. I wanted to see people chasing after the Word of God with that same intensity, hooked on Him in a way they couldn't put it down. My calling wasn't just about me; it was about breaking the chain so those behind me wouldn't have to carry the same weight.

The drought of '98 tested me in ways I hadn't expected. I had new responsibilities as a father, the grind pulling me deeper, and the streets teaching me hard lessons through wins and losses. Yet in the middle of all that, I experienced my first true awakening. It didn't last long, my mind quickly drifted back to the hustle, but it was the first glimpse of God's presence in my life. Looking back, I see now that moment was a seed.

That seed would grow into a calling not just to preach His Word, but to be an example for those still in the struggle, to show them a way out through God's truth. Because while there could always be a drought in the work of the streets, there would never be a drought in God's vineyard.

measure me out eieght

Separate $4\frac{1}{2}$

1. Four and a baby $4\frac{1}{2}$
2. Four and a baby $4\frac{1}{2}$
3. Four and a baby $4\frac{1}{2}$
4. Four and a baby $4\frac{1}{2}$
5. Four and a baby $4\frac{1}{2}$
6. Four and a baby $4\frac{1}{2}$
7. Four and a baby $4\frac{1}{2}$
8. Four and a baby $+4\frac{1}{2}$
9. Now add them all up 32 8
10. 32 8/2 is a improper Fraction
11. So $2\overline{)8}$ = 4, 8
12. Whats 32+4 $32 + 4 = 36$

36 a whole number, but 36 also a D-boy dream number

Exhibit (A) Lil Z Fraction Lesson

Chapter 5:
"Heir to the Trap"

"Born into the hustle, reborn in hope."
Dr Larry Powell

The drought of '98 left its mark on me. Fatherhood, close calls, and the constant pull of the streets showed me how fragile life in the trap really was. Yet even with those warnings, I wasn't ready to let go. Every glimpse of God's presence was pushed to the back of my mind, and the grind took over again. By the time the new millennium came around, I had gone from a hungry hustler on the block to being seen as an heir to the hustle itself. The weight was heavier, the money faster, and the risks greater but so was the responsibility.

For a moment, I thought about giving up the game and driving trucks like my Uncle Duffie. That had always been a dream of mine to own a rig and ride the highways the right way. But when I lost my license because of a traffic violation, that dream had to be put on pause. Instead of slowing down, I intensified my grind, stacking money until I could get my license back.

When I did, the thought of leaving the game to drive trucks returned. But deep down, I knew the truth I didn't want to live on the road. I wanted to be home with Red, raising my son. Still, the streets had a way of robbing me of even that.

Again, we didn't have any work. My phone had been blowing up for three days straight, but I couldn't provide what people were asking for. So, I decided to hit up Lil' B. The last time I shopped with him, I was buying ounces. This time, I needed half of a brick. He came through, but the package looked pieced together, three different flavors of dope, brown, white, and tan. I was frustrated because I wanted it straight off the slab, but I took it anyway. Like always, it turned out to be that drop.

The next time I needed work outside of Lil' David, I went to another dealer I thought had it. But he was struggling just to come up with a quarter bird. So, I tested the water with a few more guys I trusted, only to find out they were struggling too. These were men I thought had more money than I did.

Finally, I called a third dealer. He told me, "Ok, I'll be there in 30 minutes." For now, I'll call him City Bus. Between Lil' B, Lil' David, and City Bus, I felt like I had a strong enough rotation to never go without work again.

City Bus proved to be a man of his word, and those were the kind of guys who helped build the W.E. Empire. Before I started serving the block, the W.E. would purchase about $12,000 worth of product a day just to keep things going. Once I got on, the block was moving $20,000 a day, easy, in both pieces and weight. That's why Lil' David didn't mind giving me access to whatever I needed. Our bond was so strong, and business was running so well, that for four years straight, Lil' David didn't have to step outside his house if he didn't want to.

With E in barber school, Joe Ski ended up reaping a lot of the benefits of my come-up. I became more of a mentor to him, really. I was the only one he listened to. Joe Ski would do whatever it took to keep the W.E. running.

OD and Big C, two from our original crew, were the first to leave the block for prison. That's when JO, one of my off-and-on hitters, stepped in to fill the gap. For my business, JO was always solid, always ready for the good, the bad, the fun, or the ugly. Rah-Rah stayed on standby for whatever too, except when he and JO clashed. I respected the way they handled it. When their fights were done, they'd sit back and smoke a blunt together instead of running to grab pistols.

And then there was Big David, one of the first hustlers from my block. He always helped me keep my head in the game.

Arrested

Early one morning, I was riding with JO. We pulled up on the block, and Rah-Rah pulled in right behind us. Without thinking, JO parked the car, and we both jumped into Rah-Rah's ride. He wanted to grab breakfast at Silver Sands, the soul food spot in North Nashville near the Farmer's Market.

As we were leaving Silver Sands, the police pulled up behind us. Then came a S.W.A.T. team, and right behind them, Channel 2 News. That's when the blue lights hit. We were headed toward West Eastland, but instead of making a left, I told Rah-Rah to turn right on North 9th.

That's when everything went down. S.W.A.T. and Metro officers jumped out, guns drawn and aimed to kill. Over the bullhorn came strict orders: Rah-Rah was to step out first, fingers locked on top of his head, walking backward toward them. They warned him that one wrong move, and they'd blow his head off.

Next, they called JO out of the car and gave him the same orders with the same consequences. Then it was my turn. I was told to follow their instructions or face the exact same fate.

Once they handcuffed us, the officers read our rights and told us the vehicle we were in had been reported stolen and used in a bank robbery the night before. The truth was, Rah-Rah had been riding around in a pawned car. When he went past the deadline to make his payment, the owner reported it stolen. It turned out the people who had the car before Rah-Rah were the ones who robbed the bank.

At the time, I had five cars of my own and access to eight more. Why would I need to ride in a stolen car? But the DA didn't see it that way. Even after the truth came out that we weren't the ones who robbed the bank, the state still wanted to press charges.

By the time they finished processing us, it was around 2:30 that afternoon. I made bond and was home by 10 p.m. that night. JO wasn't as lucky he had a hold on him and had to stay in jail. Rah-Rah was only 17, so he went to juvenile. He took his charge, but the state still pushed for me and JO to do some time.

That meant I needed a lawyer. I started asking around the hood, and everyone kept pointing me to Justin Johnson, known for his white hair and cowboy boots. I met him for a free consultation, and his fee was $1,000. I handed him ten one-hundred-dollar bills and told him I'd see him in court.

On my court date, I thought the case would be dismissed, but instead it got sent to the grand jury. Justin told me I needed to pay him $3,600 more by next Thursday because we had court again on Friday. I had never known a grand jury to move that fast.

That's when I decided to hire another attorney, Eric Hebert, whom I happened to meet on the elevator. His fee was $1,500, but he warned me it would cost more if the case went to trial. I counted out fifteen hundred-dollar bills and told him I'd see him in court the next week.

The night before court, I'd been riding around in my old school whip, and I drove it to court the next morning. Sure enough, my first lawyer, Justin, pulled up beside me in a blue Corvette. I hadn't seen him since the last time he asked me for more money. He looked at my car and asked if it belonged to me and if I had the title. I told him yes; I owned it outright. Then he said, "If you can't pay me today, I'll still represent you in court. But when it's over, you can follow me to my house and leave your car in my garage until you pay me in full." That told me the type of person he was; we call his kind money hungry. I told him, "I'm good, but no thank you."

Eric walked into the courtroom and got my case dismissed, just like that. Something Justin could have easily done himself, but instead, he tried to keep his hand in my pocket. That was the consequence of hiring him in the first place. The more I dealt with Justin, the less confidence I had in him. He was known as a dope boy lawyer anyway, always about money first.

JO wasn't as fortunate. He had to finish out his violation time. A few years later, Rah-Rah, by then in his early twenties, ended up with 30 years in a

Florida prison for robbing and kidnapping a pill plug. I had told him to take the 12 years they offered him in the plea and just lie down, but Rah-Rah thought he could beat the case. He couldn't. Eventually, JO came home, and just like that, he jumped back on the block.

Red was now six months old, and I loved putting him in my 360 All Positions Baby Carrier, wearing it proudly as I took him for walks. Most of the time, those walks led us right back to the block. Other times, I would pay our hood mom, Ms. Shirley, to watch him. She was a constant presence in our neighborhood, always looking out for us. Even though she was addicted to crack, I trusted her with Red. She did the dope; she didn't let the dope do her. Some people used crack, and for others, crack used them, but not Ms. Shirley. She kept her house clean, cooked meals every day, and ensured that Sunday dinners were always ready. If we ever needed a place to lay low, her home was open. She did whatever for the block, and the block made sure to do the same for her.

When Red wasn't with me, he stayed out North with his mom at their granny's house on 12th Avenue North. We called her Lil' Granny. Red was blessed he had four generations of women on his mom's side pouring into him: his mom, his grandmother, his great-grandmother, and even his great-great-grandmother.

Red also knew me in a way only a son could. He recognized the sound of every car I owned, and he knew the songs I played like he knew his ABCs. Plenty of times, I'd drive down 12th and Buchanan and run into his Uncle Gary coming back from the store with Red in the stroller. Gary would tell me Red could hear the pipes on my car a mile away he'd raised out of the stroller, calling my name and reaching for his daddy. It was always right on time.

Sometimes Joe Ski and JO would have me stop in the middle of the street, laughing, and start bouncing along with Red as he threw his little hands up, giving it up for his daddy. Even now, these moments are still precious to me.

Red's mom suggested that I start spending more time with him, so she came up with a parenting plan. One was for me to pick him up from daycare every now and then. My first thought was to tell her, "You're not working, so you should pick him up," just to make her be quiet. But instead, I started picking Red up and, like always, we ended up back on the block.

Every time I showed up at daycare, Red would take off running and smiling as soon as he saw me. The workers said they had never seen a little boy so happy to see his daddy. Then came the time for his first haircut. I put Red in the barber's chair, and he never cried or moved. There were boys three years older than him who were jumping and crying, but Red sat still the whole time. The barber fell in love with him that day.

A Shootout at Home

Baby Red was different from the other babies born in 2000. He seemed more aware of his surroundings than the others his age, and he started trying to talk earlier too. One night I made a $5,200 profit before midnight and decided to go home early. I was hoping Red would already be asleep because I had just pieced out four ounces of crack rock for rock, and I wanted to crash. But when I got home, Red was still wide awake, jumping around, banging the headboard against the wall, and looking out the window at my cars.

I popped his diaper lightly and told him, "Stop banging the headboard against the wall." Instead, he started pointing and saying, "Car. Dad. Dad. Car". "I thought he just wanted me to take him out and let him pretend he was driving my car; a little game we played between us." When I didn't get up, he went to his mother in the living room and repeated, "Dad, Dad car. Dad, Dad car."

She finally walked to the bedroom window and moved the curtain. The scream that came out of her mouth told me everything. The sound alone was my cue to grab my pistol.

Outside the window stood a man with a police shotgun. He wore a ski mask, dressed in all black, and somehow hadn't noticed her peeking out. Behind him were three more men carrying AR-15s and AK-47s.

I told my baby's mama, pregnant with J at the time, to grab Red, get in the closet, and stay down. Then the men outside started yelling, "Police! Everybody get down!" I knew it wasn't the police. I positioned myself for war.

As they tried to kick in the door, I unleashed my 40 Glock; its roar tore through the walls. They answered back with military-issue weapons, the air cracking with bursts of fire that rattled the whole house like a warzone. Time slowed the sound of bullets shredding drywall, glass splintering, and smoke filling the room. When the barrage finally ceased, I ran to my baby's mama and Red. They were buried under a cloud of dust, coughing, trembling, yet, by God's grace, still alive.

I already knew the real police would be on their way, so I had to move fast. The money and the pack were still sitting out from earlier I hadn't felt like putting them away when I first came home. Now I had no choice but to get them out of sight.

Some big white boys from Metro Police showed up and made everybody get down on the ground even Red and his mother. One of the officers asked me what happened. I told him some guys had tried to break into my house, and I did what I knew to do. He nodded and said I had done the right thing, that he would have done the same himself. Then he looked me straight in the eye and said, *"Next time, you may not be so lucky. Do you see how bad this closet is shot up? Next time, it may be somebody's head. You don't have to tell me what you've got going on, but whatever it is, you need to be careful. Give me the guns, and we'll be out of your way."*

I handed over my two pistols, and just like that, they left. This was before the federal gun law was passed. Today, anyone with a felony caught with a firearm gets an automatic sentence of up to ten years in prison, plus fines.

That night shook my baby's mama to the core. She decided she couldn't stay there anymore. She took Red and moved to the Litton Apartments, about fifteen miles away in East Nashville.

One morning, I went by to check on Red. He asked me to make him a peanut butter and jelly sandwich. As I was fixing it, we both heard a loud bang, like someone trying to kick in the door. My chest tightened. *Not again,* I thought.

I guess Red noticed the fear in me. He raised one of his two-year-old fingers to his lips, as if to say *be quiet.* I mouthed, *"Okay."*

A moment later, we realized the noise had only come from the neighbors. But the damage had already been done. That sound instantly took us both back to the night of the shootout. It hit me then, Red was already carrying triggers from the life I was living, long before he could even understand it.

By now, I knew we were okay, but I wanted to see what was really on Red's mind. He took me by the hand and motioned for me to follow him. Once we got to the bedroom, he pointed up at the closet and made a *bam, bam, bam* sound with his mouth. Red wanted me to grab my pistol and start shooting again. How he even knew there was a pistol up there, I had no idea. His mom fussed at me even more after seeing what he did, but I ignored it. Instead, I went back to the block, bragging that I had the hardest baby out here on these streets, selfishly pushing aside the reality that my son knew where a loaded gun was.

Looking back, I realize Red was reliving the last shootout. His mom and I argued about it, and at one point I told her, half-joking, that Red loved me more than he loved her. She said I was crazy, so we decided to test it. Red was playing with a little red plastic bat, so we staged a pretend fight to see whose side he would take.

When Red saw us, he held up his bat and said, *"Daddy, don't make me beat the hell out of you."* We both laughed out loud. We expected him to defend his mom, but I never thought he would say that or act so boldly. It was funny, but it was real too. It reminded me of when E and I had put our hands on Pops for a similar reason, except with Pops, it wasn't pretend.

Chapter 6:
"Fulfillment in the Trap Takes Patience."

I had to stop comparing my waiting season
to somebody else's winning season.
Dr. Larry Powell

By the time I hit this next stretch of my life, I was running harder than ever, but still wrestling with the same questions: *Was this really, all there was for me?* The streets had me, but God's voice was still chasing me. I wanted more for myself, for Red, for the family I was building, but the Trap never let go easily. Every choice I made felt like it carried twice the weight now, because I wasn't just hustling for me anymore. I had kids, responsibility, and visions of a life beyond the block. To be honest, I wasn't excited about the news. I didn't want another child with her, especially not a baby girl. I had seen firsthand the effect her crew had on my block. Their party lifestyle set the tone for everything around us: loud music shaking the streets, cars coming and going at all hours, folks blocking the roads, people getting drunk and fighting, parties spilling out into the street. That kind of atmosphere wasn't fit for raising a child.

Just before Christmas in 2002, she gave birth to Jacquell Merkise Powell, a beautiful, brown-skinned boy with curly hair. From the very beginning, we called him J. This baby was different. When Red was a newborn, he wanted a bottle every two hours. J, on the other hand, slept through the night and was already walking at nine months.

After J was born, I started holding down the block like a stop sign. I was out there almost 24/7. In my mind, I figured my baby's mama could handle the kids, while I took care of everything else: the household, the bills, whatever the kids needed. She hated that arrangement and let me know it through constant verbal abuse.

I was only 25, and the truth was, I didn't have much else to offer her besides stability and provision. She and the kids had everything they needed, but in my heart, I knew I could do better. That's when I kept praying for a better way.

Then, God showed me His plan for my life. At the time, I misunderstood what He was saying. I thought it was God's master plan for my family and my homies to get out of the hood, not something personal He was calling me to. For some reason, I couldn't see that He was talking directly to me.

I went to Lil' David and told him about it, convinced God must have been speaking to him. Lil' David brushed me off. So, I went out East to a big-time dope boy and shared the vision with him, thinking maybe God meant him. He flat out told me, *"That's not what God is saying to me."*

To me, it made sense that God would use one of them. They had the money, the resources, the opportunities everything I thought was required to make His plan work. But I didn't see myself as the one. This was the second time I had heard God's call, but once again, I assumed it was for someone else. I accepted their responses and pushed the calling back to the corner of my mind. Instead, I focused on how to switch up my hustle.

One of my close partners suggested I take my sales off the block and run them through my cell phone. That way, all my customers could call me directly, and I'd only leave home to make deliveries. It was a smart move, and it worked. Not long after, we decided to shift the W.E. Empire from the top of West Eastland to the bottom. Handing out my phone number became the new way of doing business.

Moving my customers to my cell phone changed the game for me. It gave me more freedom and more time to chill out North on 12th and Buc with other dealers who hustled like me. But every hustler knows the streets don't give vacations, so you must take one. That's when I started taking quick trips to breathe, to clear my head, even if I was still running from myself. Back then, Miami was my playground and my escape. I wasn't chasing purpose; I was chasing a plug.

When I checked into the Fontainebleau, it felt like I had made it. Ocean views, palm trees swaying, the smell of fast money, and salt water in the air. Days started at the pool; nights ended under neon lights. I would walk through the lobby like I owned it silk shirt open, gold chain shining, and that street confidence money can't fake. The Fontainebleau made me look like a king on the outside, but inside, I was still a slave to the hustle, to the image, to the game.

One day, a 4x platinum rapper named Juvenile came through Nashville for a show. While kicking it with Young Buck and Lil' David, Juvenile bragged about his new Hummer and said he was leaving St. Louis soon for a road trip. He told us to get ready because *"We're going to turn up all night!"*

Sure enough, when Juvenile came to town, he brought that New Orleans flavor with him. He grilled up some drunk chicken seasoned the way only he could, and we ate, laughed, and had a good time.

I had known Young Buck even before I met Lil' David. I remembered when Buck left school to chase his dream with Cash Money Records. I could sit for hours listening to him talk about the rap game and the people he'd met. Through him, I met plenty of folks who were full of potential, especially in the music industry.

One day, Gangsta Boo, the well-known American rapper from the group Three 6 Mafia, called Buck. Lil' David nearly had a heart attack. He was crazy about her style, her swag, and her whole gangster vibe; she had him wide open.

Not long after, a new rapper named 50 Cent was making noise. He had just dropped a video, and I caught the premiere on *106 & Park*. For those who don't know, *106 & Park* was the number one countdown show for hip hop and R&B videos on BET. Every afternoon, the culture tuned in. The livest audience, the hottest new artists, and the biggest debuts all ran through that stage.

As I watched that day, I was blown away when I heard a familiar voice at the end, it was my homie, Young Buck. Just like I always believed, he had made it big. Seeing Buck on that platform, standing shoulder to shoulder with some of the biggest names in the industry, was huge not just for him, but for the entire city of Nashville. It gave our youth real hope that dreams could come true. And for me, it was a reminder that there were other ways out of the game.

Meanwhile, my phone started ringing while we were all hanging out on 12th with Ham, he was another guy from North Nashville. Lil' David told me, *"Tell them to pull up out here and stop running out East so much."* At first, I thought it was a good idea, but I didn't want my people thinking they could just come to 12th to buy dope. Still, I went with it and told them to pull up. A few minutes later, all five of my big white boys rolled in at the same time. You should've seen it, everybody scattered like the police had just pulled up! That's when I realized that out North, most dealers didn't serve white people at all. They just assumed any white person was the police.

After folks calmed down and saw I didn't get popped, they asked me, *"Who was that?"* I explained how I was moving my work, so fast white boys were coming through with $100 bills. Out North, most customers only had $10, maybe $7, and usually in quarters. I even took Ham out East with me one day, and we both agreed the flow of the game was completely different depending on what side of town you were on.

When Pay Pay from Antioch and Buck came around, I started to notice Lil' David acting differently. He gave them preference, focused more on them, and shifted his energy away from what we had built. Our business was still solid, but the vibe between me and him changed it was strange. This was the same man who had helped us all get in the game, but now he was smoking and chilling when we should have been handling business. That feeling stuck with me.

Around that time, JO, one of my day one crew members, got a call from a married couple, Tattoo Wayne and his wife, Rose. They wanted him to bring some dope to a hotel on Trinity Lane. I decided to ride with JO because I had never met Wayne, and I wanted to see if he could tattoo a Bible on my chest.

After meeting Wayne, I quickly became one of his favorite dealers to call when he needed dope. He liked me so much he didn't even charge me for that Bible tattoo. For my next tattoos, I wanted the words *"Lord Save Me"* on one shoulder blade and *"I Pray for a New Birth of Freedom"* on the other. Whenever I saw Wayne and Rose, they would remind me, *"God's got a plan for you."* One day Wayne told me, *"These other guys come in here asking for pistols, gang sets, and thug life tattoos. But you? You ask for a prayer."*

Those tattoos were my way of crying out. I had Wayne ink *"Lost Soul"* on me because that's exactly how I felt lost. On my left arm, I got *"GODIOU1."* As a kid, I remembered seeing that on a dope boy's Cadillac out South as a personalized plate. To me, it felt so real for someone to declare, *"God, I owe you one."*

Across my stomach, I had Wayne tattoo the words, *"Will I Smother from My Own Pain."* And the last one I got from him read, *"We Can't Live This Life Without God."* Those words weren't just ink; they were my prayers etched into my skin. I was hurting inside and searching for a new life even if I couldn't admit it out loud, I let my tattoos speak for me.

Not long after finishing my tattoos, I went home and got in bed. As I pulled the covers around me, one-year-old J accidentally rolled off the mattress. I hadn't seen his little body under the blankets. He screamed in pain, and his mother stayed up all night crying, accusing me of hurting him. I couldn't believe she thought I would do something like that on purpose.

I've always loved my kids and never ran from my responsibility to them. Back then, I thought providing financially was what made me a good father. And while money mattered, I eventually realized it wasn't enough. What they truly needed wasn't just what I could buy it was me. My time, my presence, and my love.

After seven years inside, OD was finally out of prison and eager to jump back in the game. He came to me fired up, ready to turn up, and asked me to put him back on. I told him to give me a couple of days because I had something on the way. I promised I'd hit him with a four and a split and even let him ride with me in the truck, selling off my phone. My plan was to give it to him for the same price I was getting it for, no cut, just trying to help him get back on his feet.

But two days later, I heard OD had gotten locked up again. They caught him riding around with weed, K4s, and crack all on him. When another dealer called to tell me, tears came to my eyes. Just like that, OD was gone again, looking at another seven years behind bars.

Around the same time, Big Dave got popped. But instead of prison time, he got hit with eight years of probation. He was the first man I knew who walked down a full eight years on the town. He did everything they required: paid fees every month, kept proof of employment, dealt with random check-ins, constant restrictions, and was watched and clocked.

To make it through all of that without slipping, without going to prison, took discipline that most people in the game didn't have. Big Dave managed it while keeping a strong hand in the hustle. Not long after, he hit me with a bag without me having to ask him.

Big Dave had noticed how I was consistently making big money moves, so he stepped in to do business with me. When word got out that I sold him an ounce for $500, people started talking, but the truth was, I was just showing him love the same way he'd always shown me.

Joe Ski's House of Cards

There was a time when Joe Ski's spot was my main holding place. Around that time, he kept all the work at his house. So, when he got locked up, it cut off my access to his spot and forced me to change the way I moved through the hood. Losing that access felt like losing part of my rhythm in the game. To clear my head and escape the weight of it all, I'd take long drives down Highway 70, thinking about my next move.

On the surface, Joe Ski and I were solid, but looking back, moments like this showed me just how much I leaned on him and how dangerous that dependency could become. It was the first peek at how fragile our bond really was, and why, later, the cracks between us would split wide open.

One night, I decided to hit the club with the crew. By then, we all knew each other's habits and preferences; we'd been running together for nearly four years. That night, I noticed Joe Ski's old lady in the club, sloppy drunk. Being the man I am, I couldn't just leave her out there like that, especially knowing she had a baby by him. So, I took her keys, drove her car back to his mom's house, made sure she got inside safely, and left it at that.

The next morning, she called, saying her car wouldn't start. She needed milk and a few other things, but didn't have the money. I told her I'd take care of it. The truth is, I always made it my business to look out for the kids connected to my circle. No child tied to me, or my people was ever going to go without. I'd done the same for OD's kids, too, because at the end of the day, the kids didn't ask for the life we were living.

So, I picked up Joe Ski's baby's mama and took her to run her errands. Before dropping her back home, I stopped by Pop's tire shop. By then, I had started keeping my work there, it was safer than leaving it at the house or stashing it in the hood. E and I did whatever we could to keep Pop's shop alive, buying tools, replacing equipment, and handling maintenance. His business wasn't just his it was the backbone for our family and even for some of our side hustles.

Before I could even pull off, Joe Ski appeared out of nowhere, walking up from behind. His baby's mama had gotten in his ear, telling him we were sleeping together. Maybe she wanted to spark jealousy, maybe she just wanted his attention, but the truth is, I never laid a hand on her. Still, the seed was planted. That one lie was enough to spark doubt, and doubt has a way of growing. I didn't realize it then, but the distrust born in that moment would cost me more than I could ever imagine, and the full weight of it wouldn't hit me until years later.

A month later, Joe Ski stopped buying work from me, and I felt it instantly, my moves slowed down like the block itself had shifted. Soon after, I found out he'd been shopping with Lil' B. What I said next, I should've kept to myself, but I didn't. I looked him straight in the eye and told him, *"Don't bite the hand that feeds you."* Those words cut deeper than I meant them to, and Joe Ski took them personally.

Back when Joe Ski had been locked up at Taft Youth Development Center in Pikeville, Tennessee, I'd taken his mom to visit him and made sure she was straight on the town. Over the years, whenever he got locked up, I'd done plenty to help his family keep going, so I didn't understand why he thought I would cross him with the mother of his kids. Joe Ski had always been hard-headed, never really listened, and had a mind of his own.

As time went on, Joe Ski introduced me to A1 and a white kid named Caleb, a guy he'd met at Taft. With A1, it was love from the jump. I respected his knowledge of the game, and before long, I was a mentor to him too. He had a giving heart that would hand you his last dollar, buy shoes for kids, and feed folks whenever he saw the need. A1 wasn't selfish and didn't judge; he just gave.

Joe Ski started serving Caleb quarter ounces for $200, and before long, Caleb was asking for a quarter bird $7,000 worth of crack cocaine. That kind of jump didn't sit right with me. I told Joe Ski not to give him that much. Caleb got hot because neither of us would oblige. On top of that, I'd noticed a black Ford Taurus following us. I'd seen it at Red Lobster a few days earlier, then again at the mall. I told Joe Ski I thought Caleb might be with the police.

A few days later, Caleb called Joe Ski again, asking for work. Joe Ski told him he was having trouble coming up with it. Caleb insisted, "I'll come to Nashville tomorrow, give you the money, and wait until you come back with the work. I need it."

When Joe Ski asked me to ride with him just to pick up the money, I pushed back. "So, he's just going to hand you the cash and let you walk away without even seeing the work? I don't trust it."

But when the time came, Joe Ski still didn't have a ride. Against my better judgment, I drove him to the hotel anyway. The moment he got out and opened the hotel door, that same black Ford Taurus pulled up, with the same guy behind the wheel. My stomach dropped. I tried calling out to Joe Ski, warning him it was the police, but he didn't hear me.

I eased the car forward, and within seconds Joe Ski came running back out. I motioned for him to hurry, and as soon as he jumped in, I pulled out of the lot. The Taurus tailed us hard. I hit the gas; he hit the gas. But I managed to lose him. Joe Ski took a deep breath, reached into his pocket, peeled off $1,500 from a wad of money, and handed it to me for my trouble.

The very next morning, I took Joe Ski to a car lot. He picked out a car, and when the salesman asked for ID, Joe Ski said he didn't have any. The salesman told him he couldn't sell him a car without it. Joe Ski grinned and said, "Man, I told you my name's Joe Ski. It's in my gold grill, and I got it tatted in blood that's two forms of ID right there!" I smacked him on the back of the head and said, "Fool, let's get out of here." That was Joe Ski, cocky, reckless, and too sure of himself. He thought he knew the game, but truthfully, he didn't know much about life.

A New Day in Court

Eboni got a letter in the mail saying the State of Tennessee's Child Support Department wanted me to pay back the checks she'd been receiving through Family First, the state's cost-of-living assistance program. Every month, she'd get those checks, and now they were coming after me for the money. I didn't trip about it. She'd been getting them after we split, and as far as I was concerned, I'd pay it back and keep it moving.

When the court date came, I showed up ready to square it away and get back to the block. But the judge wanted more than just repayment; he wanted proof of insurance for my kids. That was a problem, because everything I'd ever done for them, doctor's visits, clothes, food, had been paid in cash, straight out of my pocket. I had no paperwork to show.

As I sat there, my phone kept buzzing, lighting up like I was in the middle of a boardroom meeting instead of a courtroom. All I could think about was getting back to my grind. Hustling was my job, my only job, and it was the one thing that kept me sane.

Finally, the judge looked straight at me and said, "Mr. Powell, it looks like you're a very important man. But the only way you can get out of this is to bring me back a marriage certificate."

I thought to myself, *Cool. If that's what it takes, that's what I'll do.*

So a few days later, Eboni and I went down to the courthouse and got married. No proposal. No ring. No celebration. Just paperwork. To me, she was the mother of my kids, and we had history, but what we had didn't look like what people mean when they talk about marriage. It wasn't love guiding us to the altar it was survival. That's why even after the ceremony, I still called her "my baby's mama." On paper, we were now Mr. and Mrs. Larry Powell. After that quick courthouse wedding, we went to Atlanta to catch a breather, like it was just another errand we had knocked out.

When the next court date rolled around, I showed up with proof of marriage, a permanent home address, and the court costs paid in full. Just like that, the judge dismissed the case. I walked out free, ready to get back on the block like nothing had changed. But something had changed. Marriage is meant to be sacred, a covenant before God. At the time, I couldn't see it that way I treated it like a loophole. Two weeks later, I told Eboni flat out: "I only got married so I wouldn't have to get a job."

The Shoot-Out

It was about 3:30 on a July evening in 2002 when I hit Joe Ski up, I needed to put some work up. I rolled to his spot, but Joe Ski wasn't there. I hit the block again, still no Joe Ski. When I finally found him, he was walking up the sidewalk. Why was he walking? I wondered.

When I got to him, I could tell he was in a bad state. Joe Ski had been robbed and carjacked by Baybay, a North Nashville robber, the man had cracked Joe Ski's head with a pistol. I threw him in my car and dropped him off at home, telling him I'd be right back.

Before I could get back, Joe Ski's girlfriend had called an ambulance. Not long after, Joe Ski was calling me to pick him up from the hospital. I put the word out on the street about his car. Later that night, someone called and said the powder-blue bubble Chevy Caprice with white interior was parked in Dodge City, one of the roughest projects in Nashville.

Cumberland View Apartments in Dodge City was known for danger, even with the police station sitting across the street. But I wanted my dope back, and I figured neither the folks there nor the police would find it. To the average eye it looked like rap CDs, but it was four and a baby of pure cocaine, compressed to look like CDs. We used to call a whole bird "Music City 8 CDs." When Joe Ski got carjacked, three CDs had been left in the car. Later, when we went to the pound to recover the vehicle, the three CDs were still on the front seat with the rest.

We strapped up and went to check it out. I had a .40 Glock, two: a baby .40 and a big .40 I'd bought hot off the street. We all knew going into Dodge City that there was only one way out. That place had a reputation for people not coming back.

As we rolled into Dodge City, we spotted the Caprice we were looking for and made a U-turn. Before we could even get close to where the car was, gunshots rang out. Just that fast, we were in a shoot-out.

Junior, our driver, got hit in the back of the head. Nut grabbed the wheel, but in the chaos, he slammed into the back of a parked car. Junior was gone by then. We had no choice but to shoot our way out of the wreck and run. We took off through the woods behind 25th Avenue, guns still hot in our hands. When we finally broke out of the woods, we saw a guy we knew, and he gave us a ride back out East.

When I got home, my baby's mama knew something was wrong. I had left so fast that money was still sitting in the tube and scattered across the bathroom floor something I never would've left out in the open. I was throwing up, drenched in sweat, and all she could say was, *"I told you not to go!"*

Later we found out the truth Joe Ski's girlfriend had set him up. Even her calling the ambulance was just a stall. She had already tipped off the boys in Dodge City, letting them know we were on the way, so they were ready and strapped when we rolled in.

The next day, homicide detective Jeff West picked Joe Ski up and then released him. Now Joe Ski was back in the hood, telling me I needed to call West. I asked him why. How did he even know I was in the car? He said the evidence showed five people were inside.

Calling West was one of the hardest things I'd ever done, because deep down I knew I didn't shoot Junior. What shattered me wasn't just the case but realizing that Joe Ski had pointed the finger at me, naming me as one of the men in that car. That betrayal cut deeper than any wound. He had no reason to do it, or if he did, I was too blind at the time to see why.

The weight of it all pushed me to step back. For the first time, I stopped hustling. My phone stayed lit up, ringing nonstop, but I shut it off. Just two months earlier, I had gotten married just to get out of a situation, and now, by the middle of August, it felt like my whole world had been flipped upside down.

I needed a break from the constant chaos, but the hustle was still in me. Even when I tried to pull back, money had a way of finding me, or maybe I had a way of finding it. That's when I crossed paths again with Lil' Homey a kid from our neighborhood who was always friendly with me. He'd drop hints from time to time about wanting to get in the game, and I promised him that one day I'd put him on. When the time came, he was next up to hustle on W.E. He'd been waiting on his shot, saving money with dreams of becoming a rapper. By the time he was around sixteen, his family moved from Nashville to Lexington, Tennessee, to be closer to his dad, who was serving time in prison there.

One weekend, I hit him up and told him I'd be in his area later. Since he'd always wanted to rap, I thought maybe I could invest in his music career. When I pulled up to Lil' Homey's house, I couldn't help but notice his phone was jumping harder than mine. Lexington was in the middle of a shortage, and demand was high.

We talked about music, and he told me he was still rapping, but money was his first priority. I told him I could help get him in the studio with Young Buck, and he said, *"Bet."* Then I shifted the conversation: *"Now let's talk about this phone."*

He laughed and admitted, *"My phone is jumping, but it's hard to keep some work."* People were blowing him up constantly for dope. That's when I told him I could handle the supply.

Back in Nashville, I started putting my ducks in a row while waiting on updates about Junior's case. Word on the street was that Metro detectives thought I pulled the trigger, and even Junior's own family believed it. I heard they were planning to indict me for first-degree murder. Looking back, I can see Joe Ski's hand was all over that and he wasn't done with his secret vengeance against me.

Meanwhile, I went back to Lexington. Since I had work there, I rented a little apartment to lay low. While staying there, I took time to teach Lil' Homey the game. I showed him how to weigh and bag dope, walked him through measurements, and explained how value shifted depending on location. For example, in Lexington, an ounce was 24 grams; in Nashville, it was 28. A quarter was 6 grams; a half was 12.

Lexington was nicknamed *Hazard City* because everybody was getting high crack, cocaine, whatever they could get. Lil' Homey put the word out that he had grams for $50, and they sold like hot cakes. His phone rang nonstop. Farmers, lawyers' people from all walks of life were calling him. I couldn't believe what I was seeing. One customer even pulled up with a trailer full of horses, asking for $400 worth.

I leaned back and let Lil' Homey work. I was amazed at how quickly he adapted to the hustle. Everything I'd taught him, he soaked up. In no time, he moved like he'd been in the game for years.

For a while, I kept Lil' Homey supplied with work. Sometimes we'd run back to the 'Ville twice in one day. He could move a half bird in half a day, selling it all at $50 a gram. It didn't matter how much you wanted everything was $50 a gram. That setup worked: he made money, I made money.

But when I started driving my personal cars back and forth, Davidson County plates flashing on every trip, I knew I was running hot. Too many trips, too often. Eyes were on me, and I could feel the pressure rising. That uneasiness kept growing until I made up my mind this next trip to Lexington would be my last.

At Fat Moe's out South, over lunch with Big David, I had one of those conversations that stays with you. We talked about life after the game. I admitted I felt like I was supposed to be doing something that involved talking. Maybe rapping. Maybe comedy. I wasn't sure, but I knew deep down I had to find a different lane.

That same day, I headed back to Lexington for what I swore would be my final run. When my baby's mama walked me and Red to the car, she saw Lil' Homey in the back seat with his pit bull. She immediately started fussing, not wanting Red near the dog. Lil' Homey swore the dog was cool, saying it would be fine next to Red's car seat. I tried to calm her, knowing in the back of my mind that if the dog acted up, I'd handle it. Either way, I wanted Red with me. If this was my last trip, I wanted him by my side.

About fifty miles down the road, the dog snapped growling, lunging, eyes locked on Red. Red climbed out of his car seat, looked the dog dead in the face, and shouted, *"You better shut up in here!"* The look on that dog's face was priceless like, *"Oh no he didn't."* The pit instantly calmed down. Lil' Homey shook his head and laughed, saying, *"I know that's right."*

We settled into my apartment in Lexington. But after two days of hustling, Red spiked a high fever. I couldn't get it down, so I decided to take him to the hospital in Jackson, about twenty miles away. Before I left, I needed to stop by the spot to settle up with Lil' Homey. This was, after all, supposed to be my last run. As I started packing us up, everything changed.

Lexington Police Report November 7, 2002

On 11/07/02, members of a tactical unit executed a search warrant at 16563 Highway 104 North, Apartment 11. Upon making entry, officers found Larry Powell sitting on the couch in the living room along with his infant son. Powell possessed in his pockets a large sum of cash.

PTL Ricky Montgomery located a stuffed bear on top of a living room lamp, which contained a zip lock bag holding approximately 9–12 ounces of crack cocaine packaged for resale in individual plastic bags.

Powell was transported to the Lexington Police Department. His car was seized and brought to the station by Chumney.

The State of Tennessee, Henderson County grand jurors duly empaneled and sworn, upon their oath, present that Larry K. Powell, on or about November 7, 2002, in Henderson County, Tennessee, and before the finding of this indictment, did unlawfully and knowingly possess with intent to sell a controlled substance to wit: more than .5 grams of cocaine, a Schedule II controlled substance all of which is against the peace and dignity of the State of Tennessee.

The police report was signed by Jerry Woodall, District Attorney General of the 26th Judicial District.

Before they transported me to the Henderson County jail, they let me call someone I knew in Lexington to come pick up my son. She did, and Red stayed with her until Eboni could drive up from Nashville to get him.

What I didn't know then was that $5,000 and 45 grams of dope was a federal-level offense in Henderson County. They put me in a small holding unit and told the other inmates not to let me use the phone. My greatest fear that night was that federal agents would come for me.

Sitting in that holding space, the phone finally rang. An inmate told me a lawyer named Steve wanted to speak with me. He asked if I wanted to go home. I told him I couldn't because the Feds had a hold on me. He asked again, and I said yes. Steve said the bond was $50,000 could I make that? I told him I could. Then he called back and said the judge didn't like $50,000, so he'd pushed it up to $75,000. Could I come up with that? I did not have it on me, but I could get it. Steve said I had 24 hours from the time I was released to be back at his office.

When I got out, Steve was waiting at the back door. He told me to bring $7,500 back right away for my bond and another $7,500 for him to take the case, or I was in deep water. I asked, "What if I get pulled over with all that cash? I can't have over $5,000 or it gets reported to the Feds here."

He told me to say I was on my way to see him. I did exactly what he said. Before I headed back to Lexington, I stopped in Nashville and paid $4,500 to hire another lawyer, Donn Hummingbird, to watch over Steve and the case in Henderson County. Still, I wasn't naïve enough to put all my trust in one place. By hiring another lawyer on top of the first, I gave myself extra security. It was my way of staying one step ahead, even in the middle of chaos.

Chapter 7:
Trapped in the Fight for My Life

My pain had an assignment.
Dr. Larry Powell

The streets had tested me in every way, droughts, shoot-outs, betrayals, and losses that cut deep. But nothing compared to what came next. When word spread that my name was tied to a murder, everything shifted. The game I thought I controlled suddenly felt like it was controlling me. At 25 years old, I wasn't just hustling anymore I was fighting for my life. The block had raised me, the Trap had shaped me, but now the justice system was locked on me like a target. Survival wasn't just about making money or dodging rivals; it was about walking into courtrooms with no guarantee I'd ever walk back out free.

Back to the Hood

The word on the street was that Detective Jeff West was riding around showing people my picture. That was all I needed to hear before I picked up the phone and called my lawyer, Donn Hummingbird. He told me to come to his office, but when I pulled up, Donn wasn't there. I called him again, and that's when he dropped the news that there was a first-degree murder warrant out for my arrest. He told me straight up: *"If you don't have thousands of dollars, I mean thousands, there's nothing I can do."*

I told him, *"I got thousands, I mean thousands, on me right now so just take care of what I already paid you thousands to handle."*

I hung up and called Jeff West directly. He confirmed it, yes, the warrant was real. A first-degree murder charge. Hearing it out loud hit me different. I called my baby's mama and told her what was happening, what I was thinking about doing. She begged me not to turn myself in yet. J's first birthday was only a week away. I told her not to worry; I'd be back out on bond before then.

Leaving our condo in Nashville, I gave everybody one last hug goodbye, then called West. He told me, *"Go sit on the block, hands under your lap. I'll come get you."*

When we got downtown to the courthouse, I thought I was about to bond out. But when I stood before the judge, my heart dropped. He said I didn't have a bond. I almost passed out right there. How did the rest of them get a bond, but not me? That's when I learned the State was blaming me for Junior's death.

In late December 2002, I was booked into the system and spent my first night as an inmate on the 4th floor in an eight-man cell. I sat by the window, staring out at the city lights, preparing to fight the biggest fight of my life for my life.

Lockdown time was closing in, and everybody in the pod was yelling *"Next!"* waiting for their turn at the phone to call their wives. I sat there thinking, *I've got a wife now. Let me call and tell her what's going on.*

When my turn finally came, I picked up that receiver. I'd never been so happy to dial home in my life. But the voice on the other end didn't sound nearly as happy to hear from me.

"Hello, wife," I said. The word slipped out, and the weight of it hit me immediately. It was the first time I had ever called her that *wife.* I rarely even used her real name, and now I was dropping a word that was supposed to carry love, like it was a term of endearment.

She shot back, "Negro… wife? Now I'm your wife?"

Her tone cut through me. I told her the truth that I wouldn't be coming home anytime soon, and definitely not in time for J's birthday. The call ended just like that.

As I walked back to my cell, I heard a voice inside me speak: *"Your wife is going to take you through hell and hot water. But if you hold on, I will give you a story that will change the lives of many."*

Not long after, I was in the prison break room when a guy they called White Boy, from out North, handed me my first Bible. I flipped through the pages, and John 6:35 jumped out at me: *"Then Jesus said, I am the bread that gives life. Whoever comes to me will never be hungry, and whoever believes in me will never be thirsty."*

That same day, I asked Jesus to feed my hungry soul and to make sure I'd never thirst again. Before Jesus, it was Tupac's music that got me through the pain and pressure of life. But as much as Pac spoke truth, I never once heard him say he could feed my soul. In that moment, I understood something I hadn't before: everything I had been chasing, the cars, the money, the women, even the respect, couldn't fill me. For the first time, I felt what it meant to be hungry in spirit, and what it meant for God Himself to answer that hunger.

Now I needed a lawyer who could really fight this case. Word on the street was that a guy named John Melendez had just beaten a murder charge and was doing good work. My charge partners had already snatched up all the big-name attorneys like George Duzane, so I figured Melendez was the next best option.

But that decision backfired quick. Melendez took off with my money and with money from a few other guys too. That stung, but the voice came to me again and said, *"I allowed it to be done so that when you come out of this, you will know who did it for you."*

I'd already been to court once without a lawyer. Judge Norman then appointed Dwight E. Scott to my case. At the time, Scott had the reputation of being the worst public defender in town. I knew at least seven guys he had represented who ended up sentenced to prison.

I wrote him a letter telling him to kick rocks. His reply came back:

"I received your recent letter requesting that I withdraw from representing you. I respectfully decline your offer. I have no grounds to do so. However, you can petition the court on your own to remove me from your case by writing Judge Norman."

I wrote Judge Norman that very night, but he never received my letter. Not long after, Scott showed up at the jail, saying he'd be working with Melendez on my case. Then, three weeks later, Melendez skipped town. Again.

With no choice, Scott filed a motion for bond on my behalf, it read:

"The defendant was indicted by the Davidson County Grand Jury. The Defendant was arraigned before this court. No bond is set. The Tennessee Constitution says any person held to answer for a bailable offense is entitled to a reasonable bond. Though the defendant is charged with a capital offense, no indication has been given by the State that the death penalty will be sought in this case. Wherefore, for the above-mentioned reasons, the defendant moves this honorable court to set a bond in the above matter no higher than necessary to ensure the defendant's appearance."

Sitting in my cell, I kept one ear tuned to the streets. Word traveled fast, even behind bars, and I knew exactly what was happening. I heard Lil' David tried to refinance one of his houses, but the real estate agent he was working with turned out to be a federal agent. They tricked him into taking a $50,000 check to the bank, and the truth was, Lil' David had probably never worked a real job a day in his life.

Business on the block was still moving, but not without casualties. Lil' B ended up taking a 30-year plea. E was back in the game, and before I left for prison, I left him my cell phone loaded with all my contacts and connections. He was eating good off that.

Meanwhile, out in the world, everybody else had counted me out. With both a dope charge and a murder charge hanging over me, the talk was that I was finished. But inside those prison walls, I had one steady anchor, Pops. Every single Sunday, he came to see me, and he never came alone. He always had Red and J with him, their little hands clutching his as they walked in. I knew it took effort for him to bring them, but that was his way of showing love. Pops wasn't the type to say, "I love you, son." That just wasn't in his nature. But by making that drive, week after week, he was saying it without words. In those visits, I could see the weight of regret in his eyes, like he was carrying the guilt of how things had gone for me. That was his apology. That was his love.

I had to tell Mom to stop coming because it was too heavy on her heart, but Pops kept showing up, and in his own quiet way, that meant everything to me.

Uncle Floyd and Uncle Ricky came to see me, too, keeping that family connection alive. My baby's mama cut me off completely. She never called, never visited on her own, but she did bring Red and J for contact visits a few times, since kids were the only ones, I could hold in that visiting room. Red was three, and J had just turned one.

Red lit up every single time he saw me. The moment he caught sight of me walking into the visiting room, his whole face would shine, and he'd come running with that energy only a child can carry. J, on the other hand, cried. And I couldn't blame him. I'd been locked up before he even turned one. I had missed it all his first haircut, all the little milestones I had gotten to share with Red. That absence weighed heavy on me.

It hurt, knowing one son was building memories with me while the other only knew me through brief visits and faded phone calls. Red had that confidence, that connection, because I'd been there for those early years. J's tears reminded me of everything prison had stolen, not just from me, but from him too.

Before one visit ended, I pulled Red close and told him he was the man of the house now. I meant it as encouragement, something to give him strength while I was gone. And at only three years old, he took it to heart. You could see it in the way he carried himself, the way he tried to step up even as just a little boy like he already understood the weight of those words. In that moment, I realized just how much of my role as a father had been shifted onto his small shoulders.

On another visit, J cried and cried until Red leaned over and told him, *"Nigga, this is Daddy, nigga!"* Just like that, J stopped crying and started warming up to me, as much as a one-year-old could.

Red had always been a bright light in my life. Even in the darkest moments, he gave me something to smile about, something to hold onto. Every time he came to see me, it was like the weight of prison lifted for a little while. He wasn't just my son he was my reminder that there was still something pure and worth fighting for.

The prison counselors couldn't believe him. His confidence stood out right away. The way he walked, the way he spoke, the way he carried himself—it was clear he wasn't just another kid coming to visit his daddy behind bars. They noticed it, and so did I. Red was sharp, smart beyond his years, and he had a presence about him that made people stop and pay attention. I knew then that he wasn't ordinary; he was special. And for me, he made all the difference.

After every visit with my boys, I'd run back upstairs to the 4th floor and head straight to the big window that overlooked the city. From there, I could watch them walking through the parking lot. Red always knew where to look. Once he stepped into the lot, he'd glance up at that window and break into a little dance move giving it up for his daddy just like he used to do on Buchanan Street with his Uncle Gary.

When visits were over, other inmates who didn't have kids of their own waiting for them would rush to the window, just to see Red's show. In his own way, I felt like Red was telling me, *"Keep your head up, Daddy. I can't do much, but I'll hold down what I can."*

Life inside taught me how to survive in new ways. I learned to trade my milk for eggs or a cold slice of bologna. The best trade of all was swapping a snack cake for a fish sandwich or hamburger. Every Sunday, they served chicken. If you were lucky, you got a leg quarter. Sometimes all you got was a single leg. Believe it or not, inmates would trade a leg quarter for a snack cake. Every Sunday, I hustled to get three leg quarters, because the rest of the food was garbage. It took me an entire month just to have my first bowel movement.

In jail, there were new rules to live by:

- You couldn't just jump on the chrome Harley without a helmet. The Harley was the chrome toilet, and the helmet was the tissue you had to lay down first.
- "Put some water on it" meant *flush*, because nobody wanted to smell you.
- Never spit in the sink.
- Commissary was a must. That's how I traded sweets for real food. That's also where I learned about "ghetto dope" smashed Hot Cheetos shaped into a pizza, mixed with water from the sink connected to the toilet, topped with beef sticks, mustard, and cheese.
- On the phones, once your call ended, you couldn't call back or dial someone else. You had to get back in line.
- Never let anybody take anything from you. If they did it once, they'd keep doing it.
- Mail call was serious. One letter could make your whole day or break it.
- Most fights started on the basketball court.
- And most of all, I learned you had to make the best of your time. Marking off every single day on a calendar only stretched it longer, made it heavier.

Then February of 2002 came, and with it, a turning point. I got baptized in the jail gym and started going to every church service they offered. I was learning more about this man who called Himself the Bread of Life. From the commissary, I bought a radio. Every weekday at noon, I tuned in to a pastor named Bishop Joseph Walker. I didn't even know the name of his church back then, but his voice reached me where I was. Day after day, his messages fed me with something prison food, hustling, and even music never could.

My lawyer came to see me with news that could change everything. Lisa Naylor, the District Attorney, had offered a plea deal: 30 years at 100 percent, meaning no revisions, no parole, no breaks. My attorney at the time, Dwight Scott, told me I should take it. He said, "You'd be 55 when you came home. You'd still have time with your kids. But if you go to trial and lose, the State will give you life in prison."

I looked Dwight in the eye and told him he wasn't the one fighting for his life. To me, it sounded like he had already given up, like he thought I was guilty. I told him straight up: "I don't need you on my side if you're not willing to fight. All I ask is that if we go to trial, you say and do everything God tells you to say. Because if we lose, you still get to go home and see your kids. I'm the one who won't get to see mine." I think that conversation changed something in Dwight. For the first time, I witnessed the fight in his eye for me.

My mom's words kept echoing in my head: "If you didn't do nothing, don't take nothing fight until the end. If you did do something, and you know you did it, don't play with those folks. Take the low road and go." Eventually, I was granted a bond, though it was still too high. I had always thought the State had to give at least three offers, but they only gave me one and then set a trial date. Dwight's next move was to file a motion to dismiss, citing destruction of evidence by the State.

His motion read:

"The person accused is charged by indictment for the first-degree murder of Floyd Williams. The report said Mr. Williams was shot in the back of the head while driving a 1991 Mercury Marquis. The defendant and co-defendants were all occupants of the Mercury Marquis when the victim was shot. It is the State's theory of the case that Mr. Williams was shot by Mr. Powell, as Mr. Powell and Mr. Thompson both were shooting a gun over the roof of the car at individuals on the side of the street.

The car was photographed, and dowel rods were photographed as they were placed through holes in the roof of the car. After the car was photographed by the State, the car was sold at auction before the defense had an opportunity to do any type of independent investigation or testing as to the angle of the bullet strikes and holes in the roof of the car. Because of the destruction of this evidence at the hands of the State, the Defendant is being denied the opportunity to present all evidence in his favor and thereby denied due process of law.

This evaluation was based upon several factors. The State has a duty to preserve evidence subject to discovery and examination that is material to the guilt or innocence of the accused. Though the real exculpatory nature of the evidence destroyed in this case is unknown, it is apparent that dowel rods placed in the holes of the roof of the car might easily be manipulated to indicate an angle that would implicate the Defendant. Independent examination of the bullet strikes and any holes in the roof is imperative to the Defendant's investigation and preparation of defense, especially when you have a co-defendant shooting over the roof as well. The Defendant has been denied this right because the State has sold the car to persons unknown."

Two months later, I received an order from the court:

"The defense failed to prove that the absence of the vehicle in which the victim was killed has prejudiced the defendants in this case. The vinyl top, which showed the angles of entry of the bullets, has been preserved along with photographs. It is unclear how the vehicle could have any exculpatory value at all. The Motion to Dismiss is denied."

Not long after, I finally got a court date in Lexington. But I couldn't go because it fell on the same day as my court date in Nashville. Once Lexington realized I was being held for first-degree murder, they basically told Nashville, *"We'll deal with him once y'all are done… if anything's left."*

An old head once told me, *"A man on his knees can see further than a man on a mountaintop."* Those words came back to me heavy during this season.

District Attorney Lisa Naylor handed me a trial date: October 8, 2002. Other inmates had been waiting years for their day in court, but the State wanted me tried in just nine months. To this day, I think I hold the record for the fastest murder trial in Nashville.

The stress was eating me alive. I'd wake up in the mornings with my pillow covered in hair from the pressure. Vick Tyson, a guy I knew who had already gone down this same road, tried to tell me how hard it was for the state to convict me of a murder case. He'd lost at trial and was now fighting to overturn a life sentence. Every man locked up on a murder charge since 1996 had gone to Vick for advice. He told me, *"It's not as bad as you think it is."* I wrote Dwight, pressing him about his plans to beat this case. He told me he and another investigator had gone back to the scene and taken photographs.

He explained, *"The area of the projects on the passenger's side of the car where you were shooting sits slightly elevated from the street. That gives any gunman a downward angle at which to fire into a car. This allows us to argue that during the shoot-out, the fatal bullet could have reasonably come from someone else's gun. The investigator is also looking for the same type of car to measure how far the window could roll down, the length of your arm, and whether it was even physically possible for you to make that kind of shot."*

The investigator, who was known by the name "Downtown Bobby Brown," had army experience doing this type of analysis, and I trusted that work. When the day of the trial finally came, Lisa Naylor approached Dwight with a plea deal: 12 years. I didn't hesitate. I told Dwight, *"Let's do what we came here to do."*

From the moment Dwight opened his mouth in that courtroom, I knew God was guiding him. He picked the right jurors, asked the right questions, and chose every word carefully. He made the decision not to put me on the stand after the investigator testified. The man laid it out plain: based on his measurements of a car just like the one involved, my arm length and height made it impossible for me to have fired the fatal shot. The way he said, *"There is no way he could have done it,"* left Lisa Naylor and Judge Norman stunned.

The trial dragged on all week. Finally, it was time for the jury to deliberate. But before they left the courtroom, Judge Norman looked right at them and said, *"Do not let this man leave this courtroom a free man. He is a menace to society."*

Those three hours of waiting for the verdict were the longest and scariest of my life. Every minute stretched like an hour, the reality of spending the rest of my life in prison pressing down harder and harder.

Then the decision came. The verdict: reckless homicide, a charge that only carried a three-year sentence. Lisa Naylor looked like she couldn't believe her ears. When the courtroom had almost cleared, I overheard Judge Norman tell her quietly, *"I told you five months ago, if he's guilty of anything, it's reckless homicide."* Hearing that broke something in me. He had known all along I wasn't guilty of first-degree murder, yet he still let the State push me into a trial that could have ended with life in prison.

More New Rules

At the jail in Lexington, you had better know how to fight. If not, those big white boys would take your tray every single day. I saw men go without eating for days because of it, and the guards turned a blind eye. If you came in on a child molester charge, it was even worse the guards would tip the inmates off with a wink behind the man's back, signaling that it was open season. I watched as a guy got put in a full nelson chokehold, knocked out cold, then beaten until he woke up only to be beaten again until he passed out.

If you had access to drugs, liquor, or cigarettes, you could get anything you wanted. That was the currency. When a church group or minister came, they had to stand in the back of the room and preach to the whole unit. At times, the only thing separating us from them was the iron bars, because we'd be locked down 24 hours a day.

There was a big window in front of the cell bars. If it was open, family could walk by outside, call your name, and have a quick conversation through the glass. Those small moments mattered more than anyone on the outside could imagine.

Fridays brought the one bright spot in the week: a big bowl of chili for dinner, half a pack of crackers, a slab of strawberry cake, and a cup of tea. Friday nights made my time and my life in there a little easier to bear.

That's when I started thinking about metamorphosis the life cycle of a caterpillar becoming a butterfly. It's a process that starts on the inside, slowly working its way out, and it can't be rushed. My life felt exactly like that caterpillar: slow, heavy, dragging along, not much to look at. Being locked up made time crawl at that same pace, every day dragging into the next.

But a caterpillar doesn't stay that way forever. It has to fight its way out of the cocoon, and it's that very struggle that gives its wings the strength to fly. If somebody cuts the cocoon open too soon, trying to help, the butterfly comes out weak and never learns to fly. The wings are developed by pressure, by pushing through.

I didn't fully understand the voice inside me at the time, but I knew it was shaping me the same way, helping me break through the cocoon of prison. I was still struggling, but in that struggle, strength was being built in me piece by piece. Later, I came to realize that's why I was still locked up. If I had been released too early, I wouldn't have had the strength, the wings, to rise above it all and fly.

Learning About Lifeline

When I got transferred back to Nashville, to CCA, I heard about a program called *Lifeline.* Guys talked about it with mixed reviews some good, some bad. But there was one thing about it that caught my attention: inmates could be released once they completed the program.

At one point, I learned, you needed a court order just to get in. Later, I found out that requirement was dropped. For me, that bad news wasn't so bad. It meant there was still a way in.

The inmates ran the Lifeline program, and sometimes they would pull silly stunts just to try to get you thrown out. That didn't bother me much. I figured as long as I stayed out of their way and did what was asked of me, I'd be fine. I signed up, but before I could be accepted, they moved me to Unit J.

Unit J was the jungle, the spot where killers, robbers, gangsters, pimps, Bloods, Crips, everybody got placed. The only real problem there was the phones. Each one was claimed by a different gang, and if you weren't connected, you couldn't use it. I asked around, *"Where's D-Boy's phone?"* The whole pod busted out laughing. The truth was, everybody respected a hustler, so I ended up with access to whichever phone was open.

Still, tension hung thick in the air. As soon as you stepped onto J unit, you could feel the beef fights breaking out, confrontations at every turn. That's why I couldn't wait for the church call.

Pastor Robert Skills would come in, dressed sharp from head to toe, his alligator shoes matching his outfit, and he would preach about the love of Christ. His testimony was powerful, showing how he had overcome his drug habits and gambling addiction. His services were always packed, but sometimes J Unit didn't even make it because the inmates couldn't settle their beef, which caused the entire unit not to go to church service. Percy Lake Presbyterian Church also came through, mostly for the south-side inmates. I learned a lot from both, but Skills left the biggest mark on me.

Eventually, I was accepted into the Lifeline program and transferred out of J unit. I quickly realized this program could get you hurt or even killed. Inmates had all the power. They could set you back or kick you out. And if you were court-ordered to participate, that meant bad news because getting kicked out of Lifeline meant catching hell back in J. Fights broke out constantly. If someone got put out, the guys in J would wait for them to come through the doors just to get at them. I thought about going back to J, but I had a plan. I was working on something that might help my case in Lexington. So, I decided to stay, at least long enough to see if it worked out.

The Lifeline Therapeutic Community had a mission statement, and we had to learn and recite it every morning:

Lifeline Therapeutic Community Philosophy

We the residents of Lifeline Therapeutic Community, having experienced a consuming hunger for a better way of life, unite as one with our brothers, knowing that it is through each other that we may gain the courage to accept the painful mistakes of our past and the wisdom to learn from these mistakes. By sharing our strengths, our weaknesses, our experiences, and our dreams, we can learn together how to find positive solutions to the everyday problems that arise in life.

- We acknowledge that our present condition is a direct result of our past behavior and firmly believe that what we become tomorrow will be determined by what we do today.
- We believe there is no such thing as a free lunch, and that we must work for what we hope to receive.
- Our goal is to learn the necessary skills needed to live a positive life so that we may accept responsibility and return to society as productive citizens.
- We are persistent in striving toward our goal, forever reaching in pursuit of a more successful way of living, free from the bond of alcohol and drugs.
- We are building for our future a firm foundation based upon the principles of faith, honesty, acceptance, responsibility, accountability, and unconditional love.
- We have come to realize that nothing in life is permanent except change, and we dedicate ourselves to learning to deal with change in a constructive manner.
- Just as we came to a crossroads in our own lives and were provided an opportunity to travel the right road to personal and spiritual freedom, we obligate ourselves to freely pass on to others what we have learned.

- We further commit ourselves to being the type of men who teach others by example how to overcome the trials and adversities in life without resorting to alcohol, drugs, or violence.
- As we live our lives in this way, we are confident that Lifeline Therapeutic Community will shine as a bright example—not only in this institution but throughout society.
- And we, as residents of Lifeline, will forever be a living testimony to the possibilities of positive change and a better way of life.

—Written by the residents of Lifeline Therapeutic Community, June 1993

Six weeks later, I was back in court in Lexington. This time, my second offer came: 12 years. By now, I had a different lawyer one I had more faith in. I told him about the Lifeline program and asked if we could work something out. The court wanted to hear more. My lawyer told me, *"If you want this to mean anything, tell them what Lifeline really is."*

So I explained the Lifeline program in detail and even recited the mission statement I had memorized word for word. When I finished, the courtroom went silent. Then the judge called a recess.

When court reconvened, the D.A. came back with a new offer: eight years to be served immediately in the state penitentiary. I told my lawyer I was ready to take the deal but there was a problem. Lifeline only allowed inmates to participate if their sentence was six years or less. An eight-year sentence would kick me out of the program I had worked so hard to stay in.

My lawyer went back to the D.A. and said, *"This has to be our final offer."* They came back with an agreement: I would serve an eight-year sentence, but it would run concurrent with my three-year Nashville sentence. To make it work, they gave me one year "day-for-day" in Lexington, overlapping with the Nashville time. That way, I could remain in Lifeline and finish the program. Once released, I would have 72 hours to report to my probation officer with a certificate of completion.

I took the plea. Eight years concurrent with three, the eight swallowed up the three.

That day, I called home with the good news. I asked Mom to get Red and J on three-way so I could tell them myself. For the first time in a long time, I had an *out date.* Believe me time moves different when you know exactly when you're going home.

Not long after, I got a letter in the mail. It was from Randy Miller, my probation officer. He said he had received my letter explaining I was still locked up in Nashville but reminded me I would need to report to the Lexington probation office within 72 hours of release to complete my paperwork and begin intensive probation. Failure to report would mean a violation and a warrant. That same day, I was sent back to Nashville. And for once, I didn't mind at all.

Looking back, I realized this was God's hand at work. I thought I was fighting for a lighter sentence, but God was showing me something bigger that patience and persistence would pay off, and that Lifeline wasn't just a program, it was a pathway. It was training me to break out of my cocoon, to develop wings strong enough to fly when the time came. What looked like a legal technicality turned into my spiritual lifeline.

The next letter came from my baby's mama, full of apologies and promises. She wrote about how sorry she was, saying she'd do better, swearing she would start putting money on the phone so I could talk to the boys more often. But her betrayal came quicker than the ink could dry on the courthouse papers. Every word in that letter turned out to be a lie. She moved on with her new boyfriend, Corey, and whatever promises she made to me faded just as fast.

She even used that relationship to try and break me down. One time, when I called on 3-way, she made a point to tell me Corey was the one helping J learn to use the bathroom knowing good and well that was something I should have been there to do. It stung, but I shook it off. I told myself I'd have those conversations with my boys face to face when they came to visit.

My time was short now anyway, and I wasn't going to let her cut me deeper than the system already had.

I stayed focused on the Lifeline program. All I had to do was stay out of the way and follow simple rules make my bed every morning, clean up behind myself, wipe out the microwave after I used it, and complete the log. If you got a ticket, you might have to clean the showers for three days. Basically, they were teaching us responsibility and life skills at the same time.

I'd been going to hear Pastor Skills on a regular basis. As my release date got closer, I asked him if I could call him when I got out. He said, "Yes. But let me tell you something nobody has ever called me when they got out. If you do, you'll be the first." I promised him I would.

Meanwhile, I got word that my baby's mama had been locked up and placed on the other side of the facility with the female inmates. The timing hit me hard I was scheduled to be released the very next day. How ironic was that? I hadn't laid eyes on her in over a year, and now she was just down the hall, behind another set of bars.

The word on the compound was that she looked terrible, like the streets had finally caught up with her, maybe even that she'd been on dope. My chest got heavy just thinking about it. My mind didn't stay on her long though it went straight to the kids. Who was looking after Red and J? Were they safe? Were they okay?

The questions burned so bad I had to see her with my own eyes. I came up with an excuse, any reason I could, just to get close enough to check. To my surprise, the unit manager agreed and made it happen.

Around 7:30 that night, they called me to the front desk. As I walked down the long hallway, I passed right by Eboni, the mother of my kids, without even realizing it was her. The guard pointed and said, "Your wife is right there." I froze and asked, "Where?" because I didn't recognize her at all. The woman standing there looked like a stranger. My eyes filled with tears as the weight of it hit me what the last two years must have done to her, and what they must have been like for my boys growing up without me.

She looked at me with tired eyes and said, "I told you I'd been sick." Then she leaned in, trying to hug and kiss me. I pulled back, my heart tightening, and asked the only thing that mattered: "Where are my sons?"

She told me they were at Lil' Granny's house. Then she started explaining about losing the townhouse, saying she had to be out within a few days, and that I could get the key from her sister. None of that mattered to me. I wasn't thinking about houses or keys. All I needed to know was that Red and J were safe. That was it.

The unit manager reminded me my time was up and ordered me back to my unit. Walking away from her, my chest felt heavy, hurt, angry, and worried all mixed together. I went straight to the phone and called my mom, telling her to have some pork chops with rice and gravy waiting when I came home. It was my way of holding onto something familiar, something comforting in the middle of all the chaos.

Through it all, God kept revealing His plan for my life. Even when I couldn't see it clearly, every step even the wrong ones kept pushing me back toward the vision He had already planted inside me.

Chapter 8:
The Trap of Returning Home

You can't move forward holding hands with your pass.
Dr Larry Powell

Walking out of those prison gates should have felt like freedom, but it came with its own kind of weight. I had spent two and half years behind bars, stripped of control, yet in a strange way, prison had given me structure. Now I was stepping back into a world that hadn't paused for me, a world where my kids had grown, relationships had shifted, and the block was still moving like I'd never left. The air of freedom was sharp, but so was the pressure.

Release wasn't the end of the trap; it was just another stage of it. I was a free man on paper, but with the eyes of probation officers, the whispers of the streets, and the constant reminder of my past trailing me, I quickly learned that survival on the outside came with its own set of rules. This chapter isn't just about leaving prison; it's about facing the real test of who I was becoming, and how God's vision for my life would keep trying to break through the noise of the streets.

It was 2004, and I was finally free. The folks in the streets couldn't believe it. First thing I did was call my probation officer in Lexington to let him know I'd check in the next day. Then I went straight to my mom's house, where she had pork chops, rice, and gravy waiting just like I asked. After that, I needed to see Red and J. They'd been staying with their mother and sometimes with Lil' Granny. Seeing how much they'd grown how sharp Red was, how different J's personality had filled me with pride but also reminded me of all the moments I had missed.

Before the day ended, I picked up the phone to call Pastor Skills. I didn't want money, favors, or a handout; I wanted to keep the promise I made while locked up. When he answered, I told him I was home and serious about learning to love Jesus the way he did. Pastor Skills carried a kind of strength and peace I had never known in the streets, and I wanted that same light, that same love, to take root in me.

I needed to rest because the next morning I had to drive down to West Tennessee to get my probation transferred from Henderson County to Davidson. But that first night out of prison, sleep wouldn't come. My mind was racing, thanking God for bringing me out, yet already wondering how I would provide for my kids now that I was back. The hours flew by, and before I knew it, dawn had broken. I finally felt sleepy just as it was time to hit the highway.

With the window rolled down and the wind in my face, I pushed through the fatigue, speeding to stay awake. Not long after, blue lights lit up behind me. A state trooper pulled me over and handed me a $287 ticket. I shook my head, fresh out of prison, and was already getting hit with fines.

When I finally made it to Henderson County, I walked into my probation officer's office, introduced myself, and watched him study me before saying he was glad to finally put a face with the name. He took my picture, got my paperwork started, and explained the process. Before I left, I mentioned being pulled over on the way. He simply told me to make sure I handled it, no excuses. Back in Nashville, I checked in within the 72 hours required under my new intensive probation. Unlike standard probation, intensive probation came with tighter restrictions, closer supervision, random checks, and strict curfews. My probation officer made it clear: I had to be in the house every night by 7 p.m. Freedom had come, but it came with strings attached.

The house phone rang it was Eboni, my baby's mama. I hung up. An hour later, it rang again. Same number. This time, she was calling from jail, saying she had a court date coming up and wanted me to speak on her behalf. I laughed and said, "I wish I would! Go on and enjoy that cold bologna in the morning."

By then, the only connection between us was Red and J. Parenting tied us together, but marriage didn't. Whatever friendship we once had was fading fast, and as the boys grew, our bond grew thinner too. Truthfully, I had no interest in helping her. She hadn't been there for me when I was locked up, she didn't answer my calls, didn't visit. Now she wanted me to show up for her. My attitude was, *you went on with your life while I was down, so let me go on with mine.* Ironically, she'd gotten locked up the day before I was released.

I turned my focus back to my own business. That ticket from the state trooper was still hanging over me. I bought a money order, filled in my name and address on the envelope, and left the rest blank. In my mind, I figured Lexington's courts loved pushing paper so much that they could finish it for me. I filed the receipt away like my mom always taught me. Two months later, a clerk from the Lexington County Police Department called, threatening to suspend my license for an unpaid ticket. I was stunned. When they asked for my name and driver's license number, I explained I'd mailed a money order months ago. They asked if I could prove it. I put a trace on it, and sure enough, it came back showing someone named Rebecca Harries had cashed it.

I called Amy, the woman I had spoken to earlier in Lexington, and asked if she knew a Rebecca Harries. She said yes. I told her that Rebecca had cashed my money order two months ago. My mom faxed a copy of the receipt over to Amy for me. She called back almost immediately and said, "I'll fix this, Mr. Powell. Your license is good. Don't worry." Turns out, Rebecca Harries—an employee working right inside the Lexington courthouse office saw my unaddressed money order, wrote her own name on it, and pocketed the cash. She cashed it for herself and never entered my payment into the system, making it look like I hadn't paid at all. She worked for the courthouse and still had the nerve to pull something like that. I never found out what happened to her, but they cleared my record and fixed my payment history.

Readjusting To Home Life

Whenever I visited my boys, they were usually at Eboni's mom's house Lil' Granny's or sometimes she'd bring them to see me at my mom's. One time, when they were with me, Red and J needed something from Eboni's place, so I asked her sister for the key. Red and I went over there, and as soon as we walked in, it looked like an after-hours party spot. I noticed a few pairs of men's Air Force Ones and some clothes lying around. I asked Red who the stuff belonged to. He didn't hesitate:

"Daddy, that's that nigga Corey's. Let's throw that shit away. I don't like that nigga anyway."

I couldn't help but fall out laughing. Red hadn't changed a bit. Even at his young age, he could read the room better than most grown men. My baby's mama had been locked up for about two months by then, and later that night she asked again if I would come to court for her. I told her flat out, "I saw how you've been living." That was the end of the conversation.

The next morning, I was trying to sleep in when I heard a voice say, *"Get up and iron your clothes because you're going to court."* I brushed it off, knowing I didn't have any court dates. I rolled back over. A second time the voice came: *"Get up and put on some clothes, you're going to court."* I laughed to myself, thinking, *You must be crazy,* and closed my eyes again. But then came the third time and this time, the way it hit my spirit, I knew I had better get up.

Still confused, I picked up the phone and called Lil' Granny to see what was happening. She told me she and Eboni's sisters were just about to head to court. Eboni was scheduled to be in Judge Cheryl Blackburn's courtroom. "Judge Blackburn was known in Nashville for being tough—some even said unnecessarily harsh. She didn't play with anybody's case, no matter your race, background, or circumstances."

I decided to go. When I walked down the courthouse hallway, I spotted Eboni's family huddled up, talking to her lawyer. I gave them a moment to finish and head back in before I slipped inside. I sat down quietly in the middle of the courtroom. Not long after, they called her name:

"Eboni Powell."

Within 20 minutes, the D.A. wasted no time laying out the case against her. They explained why her probation violation should be enforced. This was her second time being caught with drugs in her system, and now she'd been pulled over for DUI without a license. The courtroom went silent, all eyes waiting for her lawyer to respond. But when her lawyer finally spoke, it was clear she hadn't prepared a thing. She had nothing to offer in Eboni's defense. It was plain as day the judge would enforce the sentence, and Eboni would be gone for the next 18 months.

The State rested its case. Judge Blackburn leaned forward and asked if the defense had anything else. Silence fell again, heavy and absolute. You could hear a pin drop.

That's when that same voice from earlier that morning whispered to me again: *"Raise your hand."*

I thought, *For what? Do you know whose courtroom this is?*

But the voice didn't waver. *"Raise your hand."*

Slowly, I raised my hand. Judge Blackburn's sharp eyes caught mine and she said, "Yes, sir?"

I asked the voice, *Now what?*

It answered: *"Ask her if you can take the stand."*

So I did.

The judge paused, then nodded. "Who are you?" she asked.

Standing tall, I answered, "I'm Mr. Powell, the defendant's husband."

I began to speak, and something came over me, a strength I knew wasn't mine. "Your honor, I just returned home two weeks ago after serving two years in prison. I'm still tired from fighting for my life in a trial inside Judge Seth Norman's courtroom only months ago. The day before I got out, my wife was locked up. We have two sons together, and I can't afford to work and pay a babysitter. I need her at home."

I continued with conviction: "I've been attending recovery meetings twice a week not for myself, but to pray with and for others. I've been walking with friends who've battled cocaine addiction, listening to their stories, praying for them, sponsoring them, and seeking ways to build my ministry. I believe she can recover too, if she has the right support."

"I have a driver's license, a job, and I will take responsibility for making sure she gets both a job and goes to her recovery meetings. I also take responsibility for leaving my family out here by themselves for so long. That absence caused damage, and I can't deny it. But I'm here now, and I'm asking this court to please give my wife a second chance. She has a support system behind her, and I promise to do my part." When I finished speaking, the courtroom shifted. People were wiping tears, and some even cheered hoping for her freedom. It was one of those moments where I knew it wasn't just me talking; it was God speaking through me.

Judge Blackburn leaned back, almost stunned at herself. Then she said, "I don't know why I'm about to do this, but ma'am, you're going home today. However, you will wear an ankle bracelet." Before I walked out of the courtroom, I pulled her family aside and made it clear: Eboni couldn't stay with me. I told them they needed to step up and work everything out for her moving forward.

I kept going to AA and NA meetings—not because I ever used, but because I prayed for people there. My recovery wasn't about drugs or alcohol; it was about hustling. My addiction was the streets, the rush of making money fast. That was my jones. Later, I would even call it HA—Hustlers Anonymous because that's exactly what I needed to recover from. Eboni got released that day. She thanked me for standing up and speaking for her.

The next day, she called and asked me to come to Lil' Granny's house. I told her straight up, "If it's not about Red and J, I don't want to hear it." She tried to convince me, saying everyone was coming over for the 4th of July and I should at least come by and grab a plate. But I stayed away. For me, distance was better.

Employment The Old School Way

Pops had started his own mulch business, and it was doing well. I began working part-time with him and part-time with my Uncle Ricky, who ran a moving company. At the same time, I kept trying to reach out to Pastor Skills, but he never answered or returned my calls. I thought to myself, *Oh well. Maybe God is just keeping Pastor busy. Maybe I'll run into him again one day.*

Pops didn't believe in taking a day off. Holiday or not, he fired up that mulch truck every morning and went looking for work. On a good day, he could make anywhere from $400 to $1,500. Of course, about $300 of that would go straight back into mulch and gas, but that didn't slow him down. Pops had always been a hustler, though customer service wasn't his strong suit.

Ricky Pop's son from Florida had recently come up to Nashville to work with us on the mulch truck. To give us some kind of connection with him, Pops had E and me believing Ricky could hoop. He told us Ricky had played ball for some college down in Florida. We liked the sound of that. The thought of having a brother from Florida who could ball had us bragging at the lil park in North Nashville. We talked big to a guy named Frankie, saying, "Just wait until our brother gets here, he's going to dunk all over you."

But when Ricky finally showed up and we got him on the neighborhood courts, reality hit. He could barely hit a layup! We had to back off all that bragging real quick. Looking back, I think Pops just told us that story hoping it would help us welcome Ricky in and truthfully, it worked.

Ricky was sharp never missed a beat and had a gift for making people feel comfortable. He could sell water to a fish in the middle of the ocean. When it came to dealing with customers, Pops should've let Ricky handle all the talking and negotiating, because Ricky had that natural salesman's touch. But when it came to his business and his money, Pops always wanted the final word. Ricky would close out a job by accepting a check for payment—back before electronic banking was common and Pops would lose it, insisting the customer pay in cash on the spot. I hated those moments.

Most of our mulch jobs were one-and-done, but I started to see mulch like a dope pack it could be flipped if you worked hard enough. It was back-breaking compared to the streets, but it paid. That was the first time E and I ever watched someone make an $1,100 profit in a single day without selling dope or hustling numbers. We had to respect Pop's grind for that.

I even had a plan to get my own mulch truck and asked Ricky to run it with me. But Ricky wouldn't budge he wanted to stay with Pops. Even though the two of them butted heads constantly, Ricky was loyal. If Pops needed something, Ricky would make it happen. One time, Pops said he needed a big air compressor for his shop. The very next morning, Ricky pulled up with one brand-new. To this day, I don't know how he pulled that off. You'd think with him being from Florida, Ricky might've had some kind of dope hustle in him, but that wasn't his lane. His game was more of a white-collar hustle.

Eventually, I left Pops' mulch business and committed full-time to Uncle Ricky's residential moving company. That business was booming, and it opened doors I'd never seen before. Uncle Ricky had contracts through a company called Stars Moving, and when they called, it always meant a good week. We were moving families into luxury homes in the Governors Club, a premier private golf community, and pulling in $8,500 in just one week. We got a contract with Laurel Brooke in Franklin the same way, another gated community filled with money. One week, after moving supermodel Niki Taylor, I walked away with a $1,200 check, and she followed it up by tipping everyone on the crew. That was the kind of money that showed me there were other ways to win.

One day, we were sent to move furniture out of a Tennessee Titans player's house. The moving company never told us the identity of the client beforehand we usually didn't know whose home we were in until we spotted a family photo or the celebrity themselves happened to be around. Most times, we dealt strictly with their personal assistants.

This time, the assistant was a woman named Kelly. She wanted five couches removed and reupholstered snakeskin included. We only had four guys on the crew, but we jumped in and tried. The first couch wouldn't budge. Two more guys joined in, and still, it wouldn't move. Finally, Uncle Ricky was called to send reinforcements, and only then were we able to get the couches loaded one by one. To this day, I've wondered if there was something sewn inside those couches, because no furniture had ever felt that heavy.

When we got inside the house, I spotted a St. Louis Rams helmet sitting next to a framed photo of Kevin Carter. That's when it clicked. We were in *his* house the same Kevin Carter who had helped beat the Titans in Super Bowl XXXIV. And judging by the writing on the back of that helmet, it was probably the one he wore in the game. I can still remember how bad that loss stung for Tennessee.

Later that night, Kelly called Uncle Ricky asking if anyone had seen Kevin's credit card. Uncle Ricky bristled at the question, but he asked all of us if we'd seen it. We all said no, and I meant it credit cards weren't my thing. Three days later, while cleaning out the moving truck and folding blankets, the missing credit card slipped out of one of the pads we'd used.

That was it for me. I never worked for my uncle again after that. We didn't even talk about it, because I knew he didn't really believe I'd taken it but the situation left a bad taste in my mouth. The Titans losing that Super Bowl was one thing, but there was no way I was about to risk my probation or my freedom over somebody else's credit card. To this day, I don't know who took it or how it ended up in those blankets.

That job with my uncle had its share of excitement, but after the credit card incident, I knew I needed different employment. Walking away meant stepping into the unknown I had to figure out another way to put food on the table. For the first time since getting out, I felt the weight of not knowing how I'd make sure my kids ate every night.

By then, my baby's mama had rented an apartment across the street from Lil' Granny's house. It was so close that her ankle bracelet wouldn't even go off. Eventually, I moved out of my mother's house and back in with her not for the relationship, but because I believed a man should be under the same roof as his children. I wanted to be present, to make things right for them in a way I hadn't before.

J was going to daycare on 16th Avenue, and every morning I carried him inside because he refused to let his new shoes touch the ground. One morning, we were halfway there when he realized we'd forgotten to brush his teeth. He begged me to turn around. At first, I brushed it off, told him he'd be fine for the day. But when his eyes welled up and tears started streaming, I turned that car around. That was J he had a pretty-boy swagger, much like my father. If something meant getting his hands dirty, he'd rather not do it. But when it came to running, that boy had stamina for days. At the park, everyone else would tap out after a few laps, and J would keep pushing, running circles around them like he was training for a marathon. His determination reminded me that greatness was in him, and it stirred something in me too.

But even as I watched J shine, reality pressed hard. I had been home seven months with legitimate work behind me, yet the money wasn't stretching far enough. Providing for my family while paying that $35 probation fee every month was a constant balancing act. My parole officer was cool he didn't put me on intense probation as long as I paid him on time. That freedom let me come and go as I pleased. Still, while my sons were growing and giving me reasons to push forward, the streets whispered their old promise in my ear: fast money, no waiting.

I still read my Bible, but not as much. And the less I fed my spirit, the louder those whispers got. Every time I saw J's smile or Red's dance moves, I felt the need to stay away from the streets, to keep myself from falling back into the hustle. But every time the bills piled up, the temptation to return grew stronger. It was a tug-of-war inside me, my kids pulling me toward the man I wanted to be, and the streets pulling me back into the trap I thought I had left behind.

Back In The Game Again

Without enough income coming in, only low-wage jobs were available for convicted felons, and having a probation fee every month along with rent, food, and other necessities, I decided I may need to pick that pack back up and start selling again. I was a working man, but being a convicted felon made it hard for me to provide legally for my family. I could feel the invisible weight of the words from my Lifeline commitment, but the need to provide adequately for my family bore down even heavier. The burden of providing was a major stressor and became a trigger because I knew how, in two or three hours, I could wipe out a couple of months' needs. And…that's the decision that I made.

I started a partnership with an older guy I had helped get into the game a few years ago. He told me he had been holding 28 ounces of that pure uncut because he couldn't sell it. He didn't have the clientele to move the 28 ounces. Lil' David was locked up, bills were due, and my kids needed to eat. Just before I got locked up, I had given my phone to E. Once I decided to move those 28 ounces, I got my phone with all my client contacts back from E and made those 28 ounces disappear, selling it all in what I thought was record time. Within 72 hours, I walked away with a $9,500 profit and just like that, I was back in the game.

I had done just like the inmates at CCA had predicted, "You're getting back in the game once you get out." The words of my passionate commitment to Judge Blackburn had evaporated into just intention. But still, I didn't stop reading my Bible. Fat Boy started running with me now. I went and got a quarter bird of hard that we had hidden in the microwave. Big Dave was also with us. I went to a gas station on Douglas and while we were stopped, two Metro officers pulled up. I knew they were looking at me because as soon as I pulled off the lot, they pulled out behind me. I hit the gas, and the officer hit his blue lights. As soon as I pulled over, they snatched me out of my truck, but they didn't find anything. They pulled Big David out also, but they didn't find anything. Finally, they pulled Fat Boy out and they didn't find anything.

While they searched my truck I thought, *I'm gone for real this time.* After an hour they found nothing, so they had to let us go. As we got down the street, Fat Boy revealed he had hidden 252 grams under his stomach the entire time. He had everybody's number in the city for work and pills. He should've gone further in the game than he did. After that quick thinking in the moment, I offered again to level his game up, but I believe deep down he was uncomfortable with going as far as I was willing to go.

That night, after it was all over, I sat back and thought about how close I had come to losing my freedom again. The streets had given me quick money, but they also came with risks that could end everything in an instant. I was moving fast, chasing a life I knew deep down was never going to last but, in that moment, survival for me and my kids outweighed everything else.

I tried to do things differently this time, put my cousin Mane on, so I wouldn't be the only one taking the heat. I gave him a bigger cut and asked him to take some of the risk. But Mane didn't catch on. He gave the hard away more than he sold it. I showed him how to move product, how to weigh and bag, but he kept handing it out. Like Derez De'Shon said in *"Hardaway"*:

I took the harder way yeah
Didn't know how to sell crack
I was giving that hard away.

Mane was giving that hard away.

I tried to spend more time with my kids while I was back in the game, but the more they were around me, the more they saw the life I was living. They watched me sell to dope fiends, weigh and prepare packs, count stacks, and talk business. They saw the weapons. I had Red and J in the back seat while I made moves. One time, I almost pulled off without the money until Red yelled, "Money! Dad, Dad!" He was always watching just like his daddy, and in that moment, I realized, again, what impressions I was leaving on them.

School came easier for J; he made A's and B's without much struggle. Red had to grind for his grades the way I'd had to grind for everything. I bought boxing gloves one year to see what Red could do. After a few rounds with neighborhood kids, his speed, a powerful left hand, and quick feet showed up as one of his gifts. He was also a power hitter on the baseball field, so I tried to channel him into sports.

J was different, mechanically gifted. He could hook up computers, cable boxes, crack codes on phones, rig video games and DVD players, and he had a nice jump shot. I tried to steer him toward technology and the things he took to naturally. At home, we limited video games; too many of them taught kids how to carjack and load guns. When we relaxed, we watched movies that reflected our world, such as *Menace II Society, Boyz n the Hood, and Friday,* which depicted consequences and survival.

But it wasn't just about keeping them sharp in the streets. I wanted my sons to know The Word! I gave them Bible lessons, told them stories of men and women who had to make choices between right and wrong, between survival and faith. These were things nobody ever sat down to teach me when I was their age. I could hustle, fight, and survive, but nobody had equipped me with scripture to hold onto when life got dark. I knew I could have done a better job with this part of their upbringing, but at least I was planting seeds. Looking back, I can't help but wonder if moments like these could have made a greater difference later in their lives.

Too Close to Encounter

Riding up Gallatin Road, I saw a cop. My chest tightened. I was riding dirty, and Fat Boy wasn't with me to hide the stash. The officer was on the opposite side of the street, so for a second, I felt safe. I cut left into the gas station a half mile before he arrived; he turned in too. We walked into the store at the same time. I grabbed a Sprite while he grabbed a coffee. I walked out, started the Jeep, and he pulled out right behind me. I turned right; he turned right. I turned left; he turned left. I felt the net closing.

He called for backup and hit the blue lights. I pulled over. He asked for my license, registration, and proof of insurance. I handed them over, and you could see the surprise on his face when everything checked out. My car didn't smell like weed, I don't smoke or drink, so there was no easy reason to search me. He asked if he could search for guns and drugs. I said no. "Then I'll get a warrant," he said, and walked off.

An hour crawled by. When he finally returned, he handed me my papers, nodded, and said, "Have a nice day. Don't drive on the wrong side of the street." Then he was gone.

That stop stayed with me. It's why I paid so much to get my license back and why I preach caution in the hood: hustling while driving without a license is a suicide mission. Smoking while you hustle and drive is asking to get caught. When you do that, you're throwing your future away. I'd rather give a junkie a wake-up a free hit than extend credit. If they're an addict, they'll go to the next dealer anyway. I never put my hands on a customer over dope. That code kept me alive more than luck ever did.

I knew a lady named Sue who turned tricks to feed her crack habit. She was a prostitute and a crackhead, but in her own way, she was a reliable and consistent figure in the community. One day at a truck stop, Sue met a guy named Ellis. His mom had just passed away and left him $250,000. Sue set him up in a room about 25 miles from the hood so they could party. Ellis wanted an ounce for $800, but I only gave him an 8-ball. Truth be told, it was maybe $100 worth of dope for his $800, but he was smoking and didn't know the difference. Those kinds of licks boosted my profit margin. I couldn't serve him the same way I did the hustlers who knew the game.

Two hours later, they called back for another ounce. I went and made the sale. Three hours after that, Ellis called again but this time, when I pulled up, he told me he couldn't get money out of the ATM. Most dealers would've gotten mad, maybe even beat him down for sending them on a dummy run, forgetting the man had already dropped $1,600 for barely a quarter. Me? I played it differently. I told him, "Keep it, pay me tomorrow." Sure enough, the next morning, Sue called, saying they had my $800 and wanted two more ounces. That went on for about a month, ten runs back-to-back, until I finally passed them off to my homie Jo so he could eat too.

Business was wide open at that time. People from everywhere were pulling up for dope. Two regulars, Woody and AJ from Carter Street in East Nashville, would spend anywhere from $1,500 to $2,500 a day. Carter Street was one big circle of poor whites, all living in homes owned by another white man who looked broke himself but owned the entire block. Then another wave of white folks would pull into Carter Street chasing a hit, and Woody and AJ would hit my line.

One day, Woody dropped $4,500 with me. That same night, around 11 p.m., he called saying his kids didn't have diapers or food. I had just made it home after grinding in the hood all day and all night, and I wanted nothing more than to sit down and chill. Any average dealer would've brushed it off, but not me. I got back in my car, went grocery shopping, grabbed diapers, and took it all back to the hood. When I pulled up at Woody's house, I gave him everything and even left him $20 so he could call somebody from the block for his last hit of the night. As I walked away, I told Woody, "Man, you sold more chicken than KFC today. Thanks for your service."

AJ was different. He was young, hungry, and trying to rise above Carter Street's poverty. I served him like I served the block, but the streets took their toll. He ended up serving a 30-year sentence under the Drug-Free School Zone law. However, he later won his case and gave that time back to the state after the law was revised. In 2020, Governor Bill Lee, alongside Calvin "Fridge" Bryant an advocate for criminal justice reform helped push for the Drug-Free School Zone law to be changed. We keep in touch when we can. Woody, on the other hand, cleaned himself up, got steady work on the railroad, and turned his life around. We kept in contact monthly until he passed away.

By this point, I had stacked a little money and felt ready to step away from the game. One night, I tossed my phone into the Cumberland River as I crossed the Jefferson Street Bridge. Afterward, I laid low in my hideaway spot a condo near Opry Mills Mall.

At first, it felt peaceful: no barking dogs, no gunshots, no fiends knocking, no loud music just silence. I could hear birds chirping. But the quiet didn't sit right with me. Nobody knew me out there. No spades games, no drunk auntie cursing everybody out, no chaos that made the block feel alive. By the end of the week, I broke down, bought a new phone, and turned my service back on. The game had its hooks in me too deep.

A few weeks later, I decided to take another trip, this time to L.A. When I touched down, it wasn't for peace; it was for the lifestyle. The city felt like a movie, and I wanted a starring role. We'd cruise down Melrose and Rodeo Drive, top down, music loud, feeling untouchable.

We ate well too at high-end restaurants, seafood platters, steak dinners, and champagne flowing. I remember one night standing on a balcony, looking out over the city lights stretching for miles, the same lights I used to dream of seeing one day. In that moment, I thought I had made it. But deep down, I knew I wasn't free. I had traded one trap for another. It was a different scenery, but the same spirit.

Not long after, I ran into a man named Lonnie Greenleaf. He told me he needed four things:

1. Shoes to wear. I took off a fresh pair of Air Max and handed them to him.
2. Food. I walked him into the store and bought him some chicken.
3. His last hit. I made sure he got it.
4. A ride to rehab. I told him to hop in, take that last hit, and blow the smoke out the back window.

That moment sticks with me because today, Lonnie has been clean for more than 20 years. He's a recovery specialist now in Nashville, helping others break free. Looking back, I like to think I played a small part in that success story. Back on W.E., life rolled on, and for my 25th birthday, I threw a block party, paid for everything myself. The street was packed, and the vibes were good. For a while, it felt like life was all good. But the streets always circle back. Two months later, Metro Vice sent a confidential informant to the block. I peeped him quickly; he was new, and nothing about him fit the neighborhood. I warned Fat Boy not to serve him, told him, "Leave that dude alone. Nobody knows him around here." But not long after, Fat Boy asked Big Dave to break a hundred-dollar bill. Big Dave flipped some money to me for work, but I had it stashed away.

In no time, Vice hit Fat Boy for doing exactly what I told him not to do. They pointed both of us out: Fat Boy for selling the dope, me for "facilitating" the deal. They had me on the wire when the informant asked me to serve him, and I said, *"Take that to somebody else's block."* That should've cleared me, but it didn't.

They went two blocks over, made the deal, then came back and arrested me for facilitation of a narcotics transaction and for supposedly giving Fat Boy change from a marked $100 bill. The truth? Officer Jackson (AJ) lied. He knew Big David was the one who gave Fat Boy that change. Big David even told them himself. But none of that mattered; they weren't listening. I bonded out fast because I always kept money stashed for situations like this. Fat Boy wasn't so lucky; he had a hold on him. A week later, Fat Boy called from inside. He said he was taking a "3 on paper three years' probation and he'd be home soon. Sure enough, the next week he was out, and his first words were, *"P, let's get back to it."*

I picked him up, and we headed toward Rivergate. Squirrel, an old fiend we'd served for years, had been blowing my phone up. But this time he asked me, out of the blue, what car I'd be driving. That was a red flag. My gut told me to turn around. But the hunger to replace the $11,500 the police had snatched from me just weeks earlier made me ignore the signs. What I didn't know was that Squirrel had flipped; he was working with the police.

We pulled up anyway. I started to serve him, but Fat Boy stopped me. He thought I was giving away too much. He said, *"Nah, let me handle it."* He made the sale, pocketed what he wanted, and handed me the rest of the money. That was his style, always skimming off the top.

As we pulled away, I noticed a green Honda creeping behind us. Fat Boy glanced back and said, *"P, I think Squirrel just set us up. Hit it!"* He was right. The second I tried to get on the interstate, blue lights lit up the night. Vice had us boxed in.

Fat Boy shouted, *"Go, go, go!"* but then that same voice I'd heard before came back strong: *"Pull over. If you run, you'll die in a high-speed chase."* I listened. I pulled over. And just like that, they had us. Three weeks after making bail, I was locked up again. This time, I didn't come home for four years. Fat boy was back in jail before they could remove his info from the system they didn't have to add him back to the chow call. The police took my new car, more cash, and even a paycheck that a girl I was talking to at the time had just cashed and left in the trunk. Shame sat heavily on me. I let two weeks pass before I reached out to anybody. I knew the streets would run their mouth with the story anyway. I didn't have the strength to tell it myself, not this time.

My sons were living with Lil' Granny. I finally called my mom, and she told me that my father and brother were locked up, leaving her the only one at the house. Before he left to serve a 20-year bid for murder, my Uncle

George Gordon used to let me help him refinish antique furniture. I'd watch him pour a harsh chemical to strip away the old varnish, then carefully sand the wood to smooth out every flaw.

Layer by layer, he would apply fresh varnish until that worn-out table or cabinet shined like new, ready for its purpose again. I never forgot the pride on his face when something broken looked whole again. Now, sitting in my own brokenness, I asked God to do the same with me. To use the chemical of His Word the cleansing water of truth to strip away the grime of my past: the prison time, the hustling, the charges, the betrayals. I couldn't sand myself down on my own strength. Every rough patch I went through, every loss, every dark night it was God's way of sanding, varnishing, and polishing me. Slowly, painfully, but purposefully, He was restoring me so His glory could shine through my life again.

Chapter 9:
Trapped in the Potter's Hands

"Molded by Mercy, Shaped by Struggle."
Dr. Larry Powell

By this point, I was beginning to understand what it meant to be trapped in the Potter's hands. In the Bible, the Potter represents God, the One who shapes clay on the wheel. The clay has no power to shape itself; it only becomes what the Potter intends. Spiritually, that means God is always working, molding and reshaping lives, even when the clay is cracked, hardened, or damaged.

That's how I felt, damaged clay. The streets had molded me one way, the system was pressing me in another, but underneath it all, I could feel God's hand working. Even when I didn't fully understand, I knew I was being shaped for something bigger. Prison wasn't just punishment; it was part of that process. The chiseling, the breaking, the reshaping it was the Potter's hand at work, even in The Trap.

I finally saw Fat Boy in the holding cell at court. He told me he was going to accept the charges and serve a 10-year sentence in the penitentiary. I looked him dead in the eye and said, "Don't take that! I can't let you go to the penitentiary on my behalf." I knew Fat Boy wouldn't make it in there; his mouth alone would keep him in constant trouble. Neither one of us ended up with that 10-year sentence. I took the charge because I couldn't let him do that time for me.

Later, my lawyer, Amanda Herb, called and said the DA was willing to run my six-year sentence concurrent with my eight-year sentence, but I'd still have to do prison time. My response was simple: "What time does the bus leave?" Meaning, let's stop talking about it and get this process started.

Despite me, pushing my probation officer to file my violation of parole for the Lexington drug case, he didn't submit it until 10 months later. That delay kept me from going straight to the state penitentiary. Instead, I got sent back to CCA. At first, some might've thought that was better, but it wasn't. CCA was like a kiddie camp, a place for first offenders. Nobody there had a life sentence, so the whole environment felt like a joke. With the state penitentiary, at least there was structure. It was dangerous, yes, but it also demanded discipline, order, and carried a level of humanity that CCA didn't. CCA was loose, unfocused, and honestly, it made you feel stuck in a place where you couldn't grow.

It was in that setting, though, that I started Men of Valor, a Bible-based program designed to help men who had made destructive choices. The vision was to prepare them to re-enter society with tools to build legitimate careers, healthier relationships, and stronger character to move beyond their circumstances instead of circling back to them. Before I could move forward with the program, I had to be interviewed by a recruitment coordinator who came to the jail. He asked me hard questions about my life, my faith, and what I really wanted. I told him the truth: I was ready for change. I didn't want to just be a hustler with stories of the streets. I wanted to be a better man, a better father, and to finally step into the purpose and calling God had been pressing on my life all along.

Now, I didn't want to leave CCA because Men of Valor was giving me something I hadn't had in a long-time spiritual structure. For the first time, the Bible was starting to make sense to me. I could read it and understand it. The program wasn't just about church talk; it was practical too. They offered an aftercare plan to help us transition back into society with real support, employment, housing, and even a community to keep the structure going once we got out. At the time, inmates trying to better themselves could land jobs with Lee Company, doing commercial and residential construction. I was learning how to prepare for employment, how to secure housing, and how to carry the Men of Valor discipline beyond the prison walls.

Still, in the back of my mind, I knew the clock was ticking. Once my probation officer finally filed my violation, the state pen would come for me. At CCA, you couldn't serve more than a six-year sentence, and I had eight. That meant every day I sat there wasn't even counting toward my time. I was just wasting days, stuck in limbo. It was frustrating like watching life go by without the benefit of progress. Eventually, my lawyer submitted the paperwork to get my violation pushed through so my sentence could begin. Without hesitation, Judge Allen sentenced me to eight years in the state penitentiary, effective immediately. I was back on the 4th floor of the Justice Center in downtown Nashville, waiting on the pen bus to come pick me up.

It was 2004. I picked up the phone to call my baby's mama to check on Red and J, just wanting to hear they were okay. Instead, I got blindsided: she told me she was pregnant again. I knew it wasn't mine. My body might've been locked up, but now my heart was too I realized the hardest part of this journey wasn't over yet.

Penitentiary Train or Slave Ship

Still stuck on the 4th floor, chained to a cold, unwelcome bench, I was shaken awake at 4 a.m. It was time to board what we called the *penitentiary train.* Our destination: South Central Correctional Facility.

The process always started with a stop at the classification facility in West Nashville. That was the fork in the road. If you were lucky, you'd be classified there, which meant a smoother bid. But if not, you could be shipped off to East or West Tennessee to one of the most violent facilities inmates called the *Thunder Dome,* where stabbings and fights were just part of the daily schedule.

Before anything else, they ran us through a series of health tests, including an HIV test. I breathed a prayer when I cleared all of them. By lunchtime, I was shocked to see a polish sausage with chips and an orange on my tray. Coming from Lexington, where lunch was a cold cut sandwich or a peanut butter sandwich with weak tea every day, this felt like an upgrade. I hated peanut butter so bad that I'd lie and said I was allergic just to avoid choking one down.

When I was classified to South Central, the bus ride there felt less like transportation and more like captivity. The way that old penitentiary bus rattled and shook across the highway reminded me of a slave ship cutting through dark waters. Shackled, swaying side to side, nauseous from motion sickness. I couldn't shake the feeling that history was repeating itself through the rise of mass incarceration. During the 1990s, mass incarceration devastated countless Black families, tearing communities apart and leaving millions of Black men trapped within the prison system. It created cycles of separation, loss, and generational trauma, causing more long-term damage to families than even slavery, as it quietly dismantled the very structure of home, hope, and heritage.

Once we arrived, I stepped off into a massive compound, the size alone enough to make a man feel small. They walked us through the do's and don'ts, then locked us in holding cells for three days before releasing us into the general population.

It didn't take long before I ran into my first problem. My assigned cell was #243, upstairs. As I made my way up, two guys were coming down. I didn't think anything of it, just brushed past and went on to meet my new cellmate. Inside, he was laid back watching *Bad Boys II* on his personal TV. He was white, and from the chemical smell that clung to him, I figured he was in for cooking meth. At first, he wasn't feeling me. A lot of the white guys at South Central were tied to the Aryan Nation, and one of their unwritten rules was that no white inmate should share a cell with a Black man. But time and circumstance have a way of breaking barriers. Eventually, we found common ground. He dropped his guard, and before long, we were cool. He even made parole while I was still grinding through my time.

New Rules

About forty-five minutes later, those same two guys I'd passed on the stairs came knocking on my cell door. They weren't looking for trouble, but they wanted me to understand something serious. I had violated a penitentiary house rule, and in here, breaking rules, even unknowingly, could cost a man his life.

They told me flat out: *"Never run up the stairs when someone's coming down to the showers."* In their world, that kind of move could be mistaken as an ambush. A man is most vulnerable on his way to or from the shower, and in prison, paranoia is survival. That's why the second guy had been walking with him he wasn't just keeping company; he was serving as protection. They explained it wasn't personal; it was a principle. Even though I wasn't gang-affiliated, respect worked both ways. They respected me enough to school me instead of trying to make an example out of me. Lesson learned.

That night I lay back on my bunk thinking about all the unwritten rules that ran this place. But deeper than that, I started noticing something else, something that stirred something inside me. The penitentiary was packed with young Black men, locked up for non-violent drug charges just like me. Whole generations caught up in the system, lives swallowed up before they even had a chance to live. Most of us didn't care about living or dying; we just wanted to get rich or die trying.

The State's answer was to stick us in mandatory drug classes if we wanted to make parole. But here's the problem: those classes were designed for users, not sellers. They didn't speak to our struggle. Hustlers like me weren't sitting in those classrooms because we couldn't stop smoking, we were there because we couldn't stop grinding. They didn't see that selling dope can be just as addictive as smoking it. My trigger wasn't a craving for crack or pills. My trigger was responsibility.

I got triggered when the rent was due and my kids were hungry. I got triggered when the lights were about to be cut off, or when I had to stack two checks just to pay one bill. I got triggered when I had $75 left after working all week, knowing $36 of it was already gone to my parole officer for fees. I'd sit there staring at the little I had left, knowing full well that in just one hour on the block, I could have $3,000 cash in my pocket. That temptation wasn't just about greed it was about survival. The system didn't recognize that. It didn't care. And in that realization, something shifted in me. I started to understand that real change real reform wouldn't come from the State. It had to come from us.

Inhaling and Holding It In

I was hard on myself after getting locked up for the second time. The weight of failure pressed down on me, and the inmates didn't make it easier. They laughed, mocking me, mocking God, calling what I had *jailhouse religion.* Deep inside, I asked God for His comfort, for some kind of sign that He was still with me.

A few days later, that sign came in the most unlikely way through a crackhead. We were sitting around in the cafeteria when he started talking out of nowhere. He told a story about the first time he smoked crack. He said he'd hit the pipe and blow the smoke right out, and nothing happened. He couldn't figure out the hype. Then someone told him the secret: *inhale it, hold it in, then blow it out.* The next time he tried it, a bell went off in his head and he'd been chasing that feeling ever since.

As his story replayed in my mind, the Lord spoke: *"That's what happened to you. The first time you heard my Word, you didn't inhale it. You just blew it right back out. But this time, you've inhaled it and it's going to hit different."* Right then, the bells went off in my own head. I finally understood.

The State issued me a key to my cell. Back then, we could order supplies with the funds on our books kind of like penitentiary DoorDash. I checked off a list and ordered a TV, a hotpot, and a fresh pair of all-white Nikes. Everything had to be tagged with my inmate number: 369324. That number was now my name in their system. CCA, the Metro Nashville Detention Facility, was a catwalk compared to the real penitentiary. In prison, a man could lose his life at any moment. At CCA, the worst you usually faced was a fistfight. We had personal TVs with 20 channels, three meals a day, and a relatively calm environment at least on the surface. But even there, nothing was guaranteed.

In winter, when it was 20 degrees or raining hard, you still had to walk a long way to chow or skip it and hope you had commissary. Most times, the food wasn't worth the walk. I kept at least ten cases of chili ramen noodles stacked on my shelf. As far as I know, nothing was ever stolen from me. But I saw plenty of others come back from chow to find their cells cleaned out. Sometimes it was because their celly gave up their key, sometimes because they forgot to lock the door, and other times because a guard had been paid to pop the lock. And when an inmate ended up stabbed in his own cell, nine times out of ten it was because his celly or a guard let the killer in.

Purpose, No Longer Pointless

At South Central, there was a service the inmates called *Cell Church.* It wasn't your typical church service run by chaplains. This was built and led by the inmates themselves men preaching to men, men trying to heal men. The overseer was an inmate named Brother Herd from Memphis, Tennessee, serving a life sentence. Despite the walls and razor wire, Brother Herd had built something sacred right there in the belly of the beast.

I told my cellmate at the time, Randell "Beaver" Spencer, that God had called me to preach. Beaver was a believer too, so when I shared it with him, he didn't laugh. He nodded. He understood. When I told Brother Herd what God had placed on my heart, he gave me a date to preach in front of the other inmates. That small gesture the trust of another man already walking in his calling felt like an open door.

The day of my first sermon came, and I stood before about thirty-five inmates, hearts as hard as mine had been, eyes watching to see if I was for real. My text was Exodus 15:22-27 the story of bitter water at Marah. The

Israelites had escaped Egypt but found only bitter water to drink. Moses prayed, God showed him a tree, and when Moses threw it into the water, it became sweet. That was my life. I had lived off bitter water for years violence, money, hustling, lies. But now I was in my own desert, asking God to show me His tree *(tree represents the cross)* to make it sweet again.

When I finished, Brother Herd and his team extended me the right hand of fellowship. It wasn't just a handshake; it was a sign that I had a new mission. Randell became my first assistant, and I knew right then this was more than a moment; this was my life's purpose.

I still had plenty of time to do before I could go home, so I buried myself in God's Word. I studied up to seventeen hours a day. If there was a service, I was there. My favorite became Unity Temple in Jackson, Tennessee, under Pastor Elliot Whitelaw. The Lord began pressing me to share my testimony during one of those services. At first, I argued with Him. *"Lord, you sure you want me to stand up in a church and talk about the dope game? My life?"* His answer was clear: *"Yes."*

Two weeks before the service, God gave me exactly what He wanted me to say. I opened up to that congregation and told them how I'd landed in prison:

I was on a mission to sell as much crack as I could. I didn't care about living or dying. But when I landed in prison, the Lord spoke to me in what I call a cocaine language.

Using cocaine as a metaphor, God broke it down for me:

"Your life is like that brown cocaine (the clay in The Potter's hand) you loved to sell, hardheaded and disobedient. Few people liked cooking brown cocaine because it was stubborn; they preferred white cocaine because it would obey and cook properly. But I will be patient with you. I will cook all the baking soda "sin" out of your life. Your new Pyrex jar will be a prison. The stove heat will be the trials and tribulations that melt you down. My Word will cool you off. I will do the shaking. No matter how long it takes for your life to 'rock up,' don't worry about the jar popping or being dropped. Like a potter, I have you in my hands; I will shape you and shake out all the air holes. My grace will

re-rock your life when you get out of line. And just like the dope game sometimes hits a drought, know this there's never a drought on the healing power of my Word."

That was the first time I truly inhaled God's Word and held it in. Bells went off in my head. My life wasn't pointless anymore. It had a purpose.

When I finished sharing my testimony, Pastor Whitelaw looked me in the eye and said, *"Keep telling your story no one can tell it like you."* Then he planted Revelation 12:11 in my spirit:

"And they overcame him by the blood of the Lamb and by the word of their testimony, and they did not love their lives to the death."

That verse hit me like fuel on fire. For the first time, I understood that my story wasn't just my past it was a weapon, a tool to help others. After service, inmates lined up to shake my hand. They said they had never heard a testimony broken down like that before. Their words confirmed what God had already started to show me: I needed to keep sharing my story.

For the first time in my life, my days had meaning. No longer did I wake up feeling like an episode of *Seinfeld* pointless, with no real storyline. Without God, my life had been just that: waking up, grinding, surviving, but with no mission. Now, every day had purpose.

I began to pray for spiritual principles that could guide me in rebuilding my life. That's when God gave me H.A. Hustlers Anonymous. It was a Christ-centered 12-step process designed not just to break an addiction to hustling, but to establish and deepen a relationship with God and with others.

Hustlers Anonymous (H.A.)

- **Step 1.** We admit that we are addicted to selling drugs. Only God has the power to deliver us. *"There is a way that seems right to a man, but its end is the way of death."* (Proverbs 14:12)
- **Step 2.** We believe that God, through Jesus, can renew our minds. *"For God did not send the Son into the world to judge the world, but that the world should be saved through Him."* (John 3:17)

- **Step 3.** We decide to turn our lives over to God through Jesus. *"I urge you, therefore, brethren, by the mercies of God, to present your bodies a living and holy sacrifice, acceptable to God, which is your spiritual service of worship."* (Romans 12:1)
- **Step 4.** We examine ourselves and take an honest inventory. *"Let us examine and probe our ways and let us return to the Lord."* (Lamentations 3:40)
- **Step 5.** We confess our sins to God and to another person. *"Therefore, confess your sins to one another and pray for one another, so that you may be healed."* (James 5:16)
- **Step 6.** We desire a new way of life. *"Delight yourself in the Lord, and He will give you the desires of your heart."* (Psalm 37:4)
- **Step 7.** We ask God to reveal His purpose for our lives. *"For by Him were all things created… all things were created by Him and for Him."* (Colossians 1:16)
- **Step 8.** We forgive those who have hurt us, and we ask forgiveness from those we've harmed. *"Just as you want people to treat you, treat them in the same way."* (Luke 6:31)
- **Step 9.** We comfort others as God has comforted us. *"Who comforts us in all our tribulation, that we may be able to comfort those who are in any trouble, with the comfort with which we ourselves are comforted of God."* (2 Corinthians 1:4)
- **Step 10.** We put Christ first in everything. *"Trust in the Lord with all your heart, and do not lean on your own understanding. In all your ways acknowledge Him, and He will make your paths straight."* (Proverbs 3:5-6)
- **Step 11.** We study and meditate on God's Word daily. *"But seek first His kingdom and His righteousness, and all these things shall be added to you."* (Matthew 6:33)
- **Step 12.** Now awakened to righteousness, we carry Christ's message to others. *"Go home to your people and report to them what great*

things the Lord has done for you, and how He had mercy on you." (Mark 5:19)

H.A. wasn't just steps on paper. It was God's answer to my cry for structure and direction. It became the bridge between who I was and who God was shaping me to be.

Hustlers Anonymous Becomes a Lifestyle

Hustlers Anonymous became my lifestyle. I'll never forget a conversation I had with a D-boy from South Nashville about the 12 steps. He asked me how I came up with them, and I told him straight up: "They were God-given."

Then he started asking about Lil' David. I told him I hadn't heard from him in a while, and the dude went on like he'd studied David's whole life. He remembered every car David ever owned the color, the rims, the sound system. He knew about his houses, the way he moved, even where his kids went to school. He knew how many kids he had, and even that David never wore the same underwear twice. And this was *before* social media! That's how much of a legend Lil' David was in the streets.

Right before the evening headcount, new inmates came in, and to my shock, Lil' David was among them. The same man who was most instrumental in helping me get into the game was now standing in front of me, serving a 10-year sentence. When he saw me, he grinned and said, "What's up boy? How's life treating you? I'm fighting my state case now." Before we could really talk, the officers called lockdown.

An old head who'd been down 24 years once told me, *"The only thing that stays the same in prison is count time."* He was right. That's the one thing you can depend on. After count, the D-boy from South Nashville came back up to me and asked, "Who was that with all that platinum in his mouth you were talking to before count?" I said, "That's Lil' David!"

That's when the Spirit spoke to me. It said, *"That's how it will be when I return. People will claim they know Me, but they'll only know of Me. People will say they had a relationship with Me, but they never truly knew Me. Don't be that person."*

The crazy thing is, I was relieved to find out Lil' David was a believer now and he was just as glad to see I was walking in faith too. I started teaching him the 12 steps of H.A., and before long, the class began to grow.

One day after class, David pulled me aside and said, "Tell me more about this teaching!" I looked him dead in the eye and told him, *"This is our new pack a new kind of service. There will never be a drought on this work, and nobody can overdose on it. The feds can't lock us up for it, and one day, when we get out, we're going to have to explain this teaching to the news."*

For the first time in years, David and I were back on the same mission. But this time, it wasn't about flipping packs it was about flipping lives.

Chapter 10:
Trapped for a Purpose

Purpose hid inside my punishment "
Dr. Larry Powell

By this point in my journey, I had already learned that prison could either break you down or build you up; it all depended on where you chose to put your focus. For me, I was beginning to see that even in the darkest places, God could still send light. Sometimes it came through a voice in my spirit, other times through a fellow inmate's testimony, and now, through opportunities I never expected. In a place where so much was taken, even the smallest blessings felt like miracles, and they reminded me that God's hand was still shaping me for something greater.

One weekend, a group of men from Joyce Meyer's ministry came into the facility and donated several of her books. To my surprise, the whole pod came together to make sure I ended up with at least one copy of each. That act of kindness might have seemed small to them, but to me it was huge it blessed me in a way I can't even explain. Around the same time, I finally became eligible to enroll in the state-required drug program to make parole.

On the list of options was a program called Teen Challenge. I asked around and learned it was a Christ-centered program that focused on the power of the Holy Spirit to guide people into the truth of God's Word. The more I heard, the more I thought, *this is it, this is exactly what I need.* Two weeks later, I started the six-month program. From day one, they had us learning scripture, including James 1:5: *If any of you lacks wisdom [to guide him through a decision or circumstance], he is to ask of [our benevolent] God, who gives to everyone generously and without rebuke or blame, and it will be given to him* (Amplified Bible).

The program was going well, but I didn't have a steady cellmate. At first, I thought I'd be moving in with Lil' David, but that never happened. Instead, I ended up with an OG from the 98 Mafia Crips. By this time, I was up for parole, but I'd just been put off for another year. Honestly, I felt like I should've made parole the last time if only my probation officer had filed my violation on time. That delay kept me stuck, and I knew if I got into any kind of trouble now, my chances would vanish completely.

For the first time, I made the choice to put myself "on the door." That was the inmate code for letting the guards know you wanted to be moved to another cell. Sometimes other inmates put you "on the door" by force, but for me, it was voluntary. I didn't want to share space with someone knee-deep in Crip business gang meetings, hidden drugs, and contraband cell phones. In a place like that, guilt by association was enough to bring heat you couldn't shake.

But as I was heading to chow, the Spirit the same voice I'd heard when I gave my life to Christ spoke to me. It said, *"You're going in that cell."*

I argued back in my spirit, *"No, I'm not."*

The voice repeated itself with the same certainty as before: *"You're going in that cell."*

At that moment, I knew I didn't have a choice. Lockdown came, and I went back to the cell. The OG walked in, sized me up, and broke the silence. "You're that pastor everybody's been talking about on the compound," he said. "Tell me this what made you change your life?"

I took a deep breath. "I got tired of running in circles," I said. "The money, the hustle, the streets it all looked like power, but it was killing me from the inside out. I realized I couldn't save myself. Only God could do that." The OG leaned back on his bunk, arms crossed. "Man, you know how many dudes in here say that. Then soon as they get out, they're back hustling."

"I know," I said, nodding. "That used to be me too. But this time I inhaled it. I held it in. God's Word isn't something I just blew out anymore. It stuck, and it's changing me piece by piece. It ain't about me being perfect it's about me finally letting Him take control."

The OG went quiet. For the first time, I saw the hardness in his eyes shift, just a little. And that was the start. In a place where survival meant respect, God gave me an opportunity to show someone who lived by the code of the streets that there was another way to live one that even prison walls couldn't take away. I told him straight up about my hustle how it consumed me until it was all I wanted to do. Rain, sleet, or snow, you could always buy dope from me. I was obsessed with making the next sale, no matter the cost. And once again, my theory proved true: everybody loves listening to dope boy stories.

But I had a plan. I'd start with the stories how much money I moved, the weight I touched, the nights I spent in strip clubs, the flights back and forth to Atlanta, California, Florida. I laid it all out to get his attention. And once I had it, I flipped the script: *"But this is what Christ has done in my life."* That's when I showed him how everything had changed how I wasn't just stacking money anymore but building something eternal, how God was using me to reach others.

We stayed up all night talking about salvation. Finally, around 2:30 in the morning, he shook me awake, yelling, "Pastor! Pastor! Tell me more about that salvation!" We talked for another hour before I led him to Christ. I walked him through what it meant to confess, repent, and believe, and right there in that cell, he gave his life to Jesus. Afterward, he fell into a deep sleep, but when he woke back up, he grinned and said, "Pastor, I had a dream. From now on, we're gonna call you Rev. 28 Grams." And just like that, my prison nickname was born. Rev. 28 Grams, the hustler turned preacher.

As my days inside wound down, the season shifted into one of the most dangerous times. Word spread across the compound: a riot was coming. And the rule was clear if you didn't join in, you'd be treated like a correctional officer, an enemy. That meant serious trouble: more time, possible injuries, and worst of all, getting kicked out of the Teen Challenge program I'd worked so hard to complete. The riot broke out while I was coming back from a program meeting. When I got to our unit, the door was locked. Whether I wanted to or not, it looked like I was right in the middle of it.

A few hours later, the S.W.A.T. team had the compound back under control, but the damage was done. We were slammed into a 24-hour lockdown for three months: no phone calls, barely any showers, and meals handed down to the unit. The riot made Channel 5 news, and they even read the prison address on air, which is how my mother found out. I didn't want her to worry, so I lied and told her I was at a job-core facility learning a trade, anything to keep her from thinking I was sitting in a cell.

I sent her a letter as soon as I could to calm her down. I wrote, "Don't worry about me. God has me in his hands," and told her to stop watching prison shows. I even told her to read Philippians 1:12: *"I want you to know, my dear brothers and sisters, that what has happened to me here has helped to spread the Good News."* (NLT)

When I finally got through on the phone, my family told me to stop writing like that, those letters made Mom cry. They thought my words were sugar-coated promises; they'd seen this story before: you get out, say the right things, and go right back to the block. It reminded me of how some folks reacted to the Apostle Paul: they praised his letters but criticized his presence, like in 2 Corinthians 10:10. I tucked that verse into my spiritual piggy bank and made a quiet vow: fine, let them doubt. I'll show them.

At the base of the Statue of Liberty is a broken chain, a symbol meant to invite the broken, the hurting, and the forgotten to come to America. It says that no matter who you are or where you come from, freedom waits for you here. But my people know a different reality, we are not free. We live like hamsters in glass cages, staring at that promise of liberty while stuck in place. We run on the wheel, faster and faster, believing we're making progress, only to realize we haven't moved an inch. We've been running for over 400 years and remain in the same spot. Free doesn't always mean freedom, but Jesus put it plain in John 8:36: *"If the Son sets you free, you will be free indeed."* (NIV)

I missed my kids like crazy. I was never the type to neglect my responsibility as a father. I may not have been the best, but I always tried. Now, I was determined like the Army motto to be *all that I could be.* I had made up my mind: whatever it took, I was going to get back to my boys ASAP. By this point, I had served three years into my sentence, and it had been three long months since I'd heard anything from them. Their mama was pregnant with her third child, and I didn't even know who the father was. All I could think was, *how is she going to feed another mouth when she can barely take care of the two, she already has?*

I graduated from the Teen Challenge program without any problems, which gave me everything I needed to face the parole board. All I had to do now was stay out of trouble. But prison doesn't care about your plans. Two weeks later, a gang fight erupted. From my cell, I watched chaos unfold, knives flashing everywhere, blood spilling across the floor. It was like watching a war zone. My cellmate at the time was a white boy serving 25 years at 100 percent. His parents were racist, but he wasn't. That put pressure on him from the white brotherhood gangs, who were always pressing him to get down with them. He caught heat every day, but at night, he read his Bible and tried to stay out of the way. More than once, he told me, "I don't know how long I can hold them off." And I'd tell him, "Don't stress it. Let Jesus hold them off for you."

I taught Lil' David how to play dominoes, and he taught me how to play chess. That game taught me something deeper than just moving pieces on a board. In chess, no matter how bad you're losing, the game is never really over. One wrong move by your opponent can shift everything. I started looking at chess the same way I looked at life: you can be down bad, losing piece after piece, but one move by the hand of God can turn it all around.

One night, as I laid back listening to the rain tap against the windows, the Lord spoke to me. His voice was clear: *"Son, I'm giving you a word of instruction soon. There's a problem coming that will hit you hard within the next week."* Not long after, the gang fight shook the prison, and they broke up our unit. Thirty of us were transferred into what they called an "honor pod." It was quieter, calmer a world away from the chaos of the compound. One evening, I noticed a guy named Bus Head leaning against the rail, wearing a hard mean mug.

"What's up, Bus?" I asked.

He shook his head. "Man, I can't take this anymore. It's too quiet in here. You can hear a pin drop. No drama, no nothing. I don't expect you to understand, but this pod is making my third eye weak. I got 15 more years to do, and I've got to stay sharp. Being in here's softening me up."

I just nodded, but inside, I couldn't have felt more different. I was thankful for the peace. For once, I didn't have to keep my head on a swivel every second. I could breathe, study, and focus. Lil' David felt the same way. I could see it in the way he carried himself. Three months later, I got blessed with a transfer down to the annex, and that's when life really started to shift. The annex gave us more freedom. We had longer yard time and fewer lockdowns, and after the last count, we were even allowed to come back outside. That extra time in the chapel became my sanctuary. One day, as I was heading back into my cell, God led me to stop and look in the mirror. I took off my shirt, and my eyes were drawn to the tattoo on my right shoulder that read, *"I pray for a new birth of freedom."* In that moment, the words felt alive. I reached for my Bible and turned to John 3:3-7, where Jesus tells Nicodemus, "No one can see the kingdom of God unless they are born again." I felt just like Nicodemus, wondering how a man could be born again after living so long in sin. But God was showing me that my rebirth wasn't about starting over physically; it was a spiritual transformat-ion. He used my past, even the tattoos etched into my skin, as symbols of the transformation He was bringing to my life.

The State paid me $34 a month to keep the chapel floor waxed and buffed, but what I was really getting paid for was peace. The annex was laid-back compared to the rest of the compound. No more long, cold walks in the rain, just to get to chow; everything we needed was under one roof. And most of all, I didn't have to worry about knives in the shadows. It's funny how those blades seem to disappear when you're in a place built for peace instead of war.

So far, I'd been making good decisions, and part of never giving up is learning to make the right choices even when you're hurting, discouraged, frustrated, or under pressure. If you don't pay the price to do what's right now, the consequence of an undisciplined life will eventually show up and it will cost more than you ever imagined.

I recall seeing an actor portray the devil in a red suit with horns and a pitchfork years ago. That image made Satan look like a joke, and that's exactly how he wants it. The truth is, the enemy is nothing to laugh at. He has intellect, emotion, will, and personality. He doesn't need a body of his own because he manifests through people. That's why Paul warns us in Ephesians 6:12: *"For we do not wrestle against flesh and blood, but against rulers, against authorities, against the powers of this dark world and against the spiritual forces of evil in the heavenly realms."*

Prison can feel like the center of that dark world. You can come out bitter, or you can come out better. I prayed daily that my time would make me better, not worse. I asked God to let my struggles strengthen my trust in Him, even when it hurt. And I began to see the truth sometimes God won't answer our prayers because He knows if He gives us what we want, it will pull us further from His purpose. Satan, on the other hand, will hand you everything you think you want money, women, power because he knows it won't last. He knows today's blessing outside of God's will becomes tomorrow's curse. Satan's price tag is always death. If he can't have your soul in the grave, prison is his next best option. But even in prison, God had already written my purpose before I was born.

I had about six months left before parole when I found out Eboni had given birth to her third child, Dajhia, in August 2006. As time passed, the Spirit led me to Psalm 112:7 *"He is not afraid of bad news; his heart is firm, trusting in the Lord."* I held onto that scripture like it was oxygen. And sure enough, the Word prepared me. Ten days later, I called home. Three times I asked to speak to my son J, and each time my family avoided putting him on the line. Finally, they handed him the phone. His little voice came through, "Daddy, Daddy! Mom is pregnant again."

That broke me. For a moment, it felt like my heart had collapsed. But then I remembered Psalm 112, and the weight slid off me like water rolling down a glass. God had prepared me for that pain. By 2008, I still hadn't seen a single picture of Dajhia. And now Eboni was pregnant again. Two weeks later, the truth came out Dajhia's father wasn't me. She belonged to Joe Ski, my so-called right-hand man from West Eastland. I couldn't believe it when she said it. My stomach turned, and I hung up the phone immediately. Then I told my mom to call Joe Ski and set up a three-way call.

My first words to Joe Ski were, "So, we're doing this now?" He tried explaining himself, but I wasn't hearing it. My blood boiled. All I could think about was payback. I hung up and called my baby's mama back. She said she hadn't told me sooner because she didn't want to put more stress on me while I was locked up. "But since you've only got a short time left, I wanted to tell you before you got out," she said.

I told her, "You should've told me long before now. That way I would've had time to heal."

On my way back to my cell before count, I stopped by a guy named AJ's cell, whom I knew from being in prison, to make conversation. Maybe God led me there, because when I walked in, I heard a song playing on his radio that felt like it was speaking directly to me:

"The more you show a nigga, the more dangerous he become to ya, homie.
I broke bread with you, nigga, showed you where I live.
You taught me what a good heart in these streets will get a nigga—
Not a muthafuckin' thang but a sad picture.
I never thought I'd say it, but muthafuck a friend,
Cause your dog be the one that cross you in the end…"

—Plies, *Keep It Too Real*

Those lyrics hit me like a mirror being held up to my life. They captured exactly how I felt about Joe Ski's betrayal. But the difference now was that I wasn't the same man I used to be. The old me would've sought revenge. The new me needed more than street wisdom I needed God's revelation.

That night during count, the Spirit of the Lord spoke to me: "I've got a message I want you to hear in the prison chapel. I'll show you which one."

Later, I went to the chapel and started flipping through the pile of DVDs. When my hand touched one, the Spirit stopped me. The title was *The God Who Married a Whore* by Bishop T.D. Jakes. In it, he preached from Hosea, where God told Hosea to marry Gomer, a woman who lived an unfaithful, incomplete life. Hosea's very name means *salvation* he saves; he helps. That word broke me down and lifted me up at the same time. God was showing me that even betrayal, even brokenness, can't stop His purpose. I walked out of the chapel that night spiritually high, living proof of Psalm 107:20: *"He sent his word, and healed them, and delivered them from their destructions." (KJV)*

During my last five months around the fall of 2008, I stayed buried in the Bible and prayed hard. I knew my time was almost up, but I wanted to finish right. My cellmate was Dirty Black; someone I'd known since I was a kid. Back in the day, he was the one everybody in the neighborhood noticed rolling in Cadillacs, dressed sharp, always with money in his pocket. But I also knew he had been locked up and strung out. One night I asked him why he never put me in the game back then. He laughed and said, "You were just a kid, man. I wasn't about to hand you that kind of life."

It was good to have him in my cell. We knew a lot of the same people, so the nights passed with us swapping old stories and clowning each other. He cracked jokes on me all the time once he said, "Man, I hope you don't die in this little cell. Your head already big. If it swells any bigger, they gon' have to cut the whole doorframe out just to drag you out of here." We laughed for hours, and in moments like that, I felt a little lighter, like the weight of prison didn't sit so heavy.

But what made Dirty Black stand out to me was his story. People still talk about him in Nashville. He was the one who fell all the way into addiction, then somehow climbed out, flipped the hustle, and got rich. He didn't get addicted to drugs he got addicted to money. He went from shooting up dope to driving customized Cadillacs. From the gutter to customized trucks, houses, and flashy cars. To us, that was the kind of transformation that looked like success. But I saw deeper: it was still addiction. He never broke free he just traded one chain for another.

I graduated from the pre-release program while I was still there, and that's when the truth hit me hardest. For the first time, I saw the destruction my hustle had caused. Parents giving me their last dollar while their kids sat hungry. Families selling furniture, pawning TVs, stealing from each other just to hand me money for dope. Husbands pimping their wives, wives sneaking behind their husbands' backs. I had taken people's light bills, grocery money, even their dignity and turned it into profit. I had never thought about the trail of pain my hustle left behind.

The prison paid me $65 a month for the program, but when that was done, my next job paid me $27 a month to wash dishes and haul trash for breakfast, lunch, and dinner. That's where I met Big Sloppy from Chattanooga. The name didn't fit him at all he was 6'4" of pure muscle, but everybody called him that anyway. He knew I had plans to preach when I got out, and he respected that. By then, the whole compound knew me as the one who wanted to hit the streets again not with a pack in my hand, but with the Word of God.

I prayed, "Lord, when I get out of here, bless me with a job where I can clean up Your church and hear Your Word at the same time. If you don't, I'm afraid I'll end up right back in prison." That prayer became my daily routine in the last few months of my time every morning, every night, the same plea.

Not long after, I received a hearing notice from the State of Tennessee Board of Probation and Parole. It read: *"This is to advise that you are scheduled for a hearing at South Central Correctional Facility on 7/14/2008. If, for any reason, you are deleted from the final docket, you will be notified with an explanation. You will receive written notification of the final decision of your parole hearing."*

When the final decision came back, it was good. I was approved. Three days later, I checked the computer system and saw my release date: 8/11/08. Freedom was on the calendar. From that moment forward, my focus shifted. I thought about nothing but the vision God had given me. I repeated it over and over until it was carved into my soul: *I will grind again, but this time, for a higher purpose.*

The Visions of My Ministry

This ministry is a new phenomenon designed to impact both the prison system and the streets in the 21st century. From the 70s through the early 2000s, many sought peace and purpose in all the wrong places, turning to drugs, violence, and the trap of life as misguided sources of fulfillment. Many of us grew into adulthood scarred by those choices, our lives torn apart and in desperate need of healing.

This ministry exists to bring that healing. It is dedicated to reaching those whose struggles with addiction, guilt, shame, and brokenness have gained control of their lives. It offers real answers, rooted not in the streets, but in the transforming power of Christ.

When I study Jesus' life, I see how He intentionally spent His time with the broken, violent criminals, prostitutes, tax collectors, and outcasts. He didn't avoid them; He sought them out. In Luke 4, Jesus launched His public ministry by reading from Isaiah 61: *"The Spirit of the Lord is upon me, because He has anointed me to proclaim good news to the poor. He has sent me to proclaim freedom for the prisoners and recovery of sight for the blind, to set the oppressed free."*

That is the model. That is the calling. True healing and Christ-centered recovery happen best within the body of the local church, where unconditional love and accountability flow from a community of believers. My vision is to raise up a ministry that restores God's prodigal sons and daughters, offering them what the streets could never give: freedom, purpose, and the love of Christ.

Chapter 11:
Trapped by Freedom —Freedom Must Be Managed

Christ has set us free to live a life of freedom.
Galatians 5:1

August 11, 2008. The day I had prayed for, counted down to, and dreamed about finally arrived. My release date. Only my mother knew I was coming home I wanted to keep it that way. The State of Tennessee handed me a pair of Dollar General shorts, a $35 check, and a bus ticket. That was their way of sending me back into the world. From South Central, just outside of Lexington, they drove me to the Jackson bus station, where I would ride into Nashville.

On the ride home, my mind was racing. Freedom felt good, but I knew this was the kind of blessing that could turn into a curse if I didn't manage it right. Freedom must be managed, or it can trap you all over again.

I told my mother to meet me downtown around 3:30 pm and to have smothered chicken with rice and gravy waiting. Finally, I'd be able to hug her again. I had stopped her from visiting me when I was in the county jail, it was too much for her to see me that way. Now she would see me free.

As I looked out the bus window, I thought about all the mothers who never get this moment, the ones whose sons went to prison but never came back alive. That prayer sat heavily on me as I clutched that $35 check and prepared to step into my new chapter.

My mother and my brother Ricky were waiting for me when I got off the bus. Ricky grabbed all my Bibles and books and stacked them in the trunk of my mom's car. As soon as we pulled off, all I could think about was real food. Prison food never satisfied my stomach I had been waiting for this day.

But before anything else, I needed to see my kids. I wanted to drive myself, but my license had expired two years earlier. Driving on an expired license was a risk I didn't need to take; I'd already spent too many years losing my freedom. So, my mom drove me to my baby's mama's house.

When I knocked, she said, "Come in." The next thing I heard was little feet pounding across the floor. J and Dajhia ran straight toward me, yelling, "Daddy!!" I bent down and wrapped them both in my arms. Red, who was now 8 years old, wasn't there at first, he was downstairs visiting a friend. But when he finally came in and saw me, he broke down crying. He couldn't believe I was home. His eyes told me that this moment would stay with him forever, his daddy coming home on the very first day of school that year.

But as my kids called out "Daddy," I knew one voice was missing. Her name was Malia Ridley Powell. She was only six months old, beautiful, innocent, with a face that could melt stone. Even though Dajhia and Malia were both conceived during my time behind bars, none of that mattered in my heart. They were mine. I loved them with everything I had.

At that point, I was living back at my mom's house. My cousin Nicole and her brother Mane came by later and asked if I wanted to ride around. I trusted Nicole, so I hopped in. As we drove through the city, Mane pointed at a church sign on Old Hickory Blvd. "Man, a lot of pretty girls go to that church," he said. But I didn't see girls I saw the church sign. Right then, the Holy Spirit whispered to me: *"Remember the church sign, not what he said about the pretty girls."*

My next stop was supposed to be Joe Ski's house. I wanted to look him in the eye and tell him I forgave him, that I carried no bitterness in my heart. But as fate had it, he was locked up again. Later that night, I ended up back at my baby's mama's house. It was nearly 10 pm, and the kids still hadn't eaten or taken a bath. The house was full of people, music, and noise. I stepped in and told everyone it was time to leave. At the time, I didn't realize

I had just broken up a cocaine party. My insistence didn't sit well with my baby's mama but as a father, I knew my kids needed order, not chaos.

The next day, I reported to my parole officer. Before I got released, I had received a letter saying Charlene Moneymaker would be assigned to my case and that I needed to report to her within 72 hours. The irony of that name wasn't lost on me. *Moneymaker* sounded like a nickname straight out of a strip club, not the name of a parole officer. When I finally met her, she was nothing like I expected tall, white, and not threatening at all. As we talked, she told me she raced horses. That caught my attention because it reminded me of the Kentucky Derby, which I used to attend almost every year since I was fourteen. I wasn't working those weekends, just soaking up the culture, the energy, and the rush of it all.

Moneymaker, though, was all business. She went strictly by the book, but that was fine with me. For my future, I was going by *the* Book the Bible. I reported twice a month, showed proof of a job, paid my $35 probation fee, and took random drug tests. Since I never smoked, drank, or gambled, I didn't worry. In fact, I often asked her with confidence, "Where's your piss cup today?" knowing I had nothing to hide.

My biggest struggle was employment. With five felonies on my record, doors closed before they even opened. Moneymaker recommended Goodwill Industries. I sat through orientation for an entire week, only for them to tell me at the end that they couldn't hire me because of a property theft charge on my record. I said, "Ma'am, you saw everything else on my record, but you're worried about me stealing?" That charge was from when JO, Rah-Rah, and I were pulled over. My lawyer had beaten the case, but somehow it still haunted me on paper. Of course, Moneymaker wasn't trying to hear my side of it.

Meanwhile, the fallout from the night before was spreading. Word got around fast that I had put everybody out of the house including my baby's mama's boyfriend. She called me the next day, her voice sharp and cold. "You can't turn my house into a church overnight. Just because you've been gone all these years and got spiritual doesn't mean anything to me. Life had to continue out here without you." She had no idea her words took me straight back to that message I'd heard from T.D. Jakes in prison, *"The God Who Married a Whore."* That sermon had shifted my perspective and given me a whole new love for Eboni. I told her I wanted to make our marriage work, that God had healed my heart and taught me how to forgive her and Joe Ski. All I wanted now was to give our kids a better life. But she didn't believe me. She didn't think I could love Dajhia and baby Malia like they were mine, or that I could let go of the past. She couldn't accept my transformation or imagine what it meant for our future.

Around the fall of 2009, Joe Ski came home. Dajhia and I went to see him, and we sat down for a man-to-man conversation. He finally admitted that sleeping with my baby's mama was his way of paying me back for what he thought I had done to him. Confused, I asked, "When did I ever sleep with your baby's mama?" He brought up a girl named Vodka. I had once helped her get food for her kids, and later she told him she was "with the big man now over W.E." Joe Ski twisted her words into something more.

I looked him in the eyes and said, "So you mean to tell me you carried this in your heart all this time instead of coming to me like a man and asking? You know I don't move like that! That's not who I am. Either way, things can never be the same between us. There's no beef I'm not holding onto that, but you've got bigger matters to deal with now. You've got a little girl to raise, and I'll still do what I've always done: make sure your kids eat when you can't." Seven months later, Joe Ski was locked up again.

By then, I had been home for about three months and still couldn't land a job anywhere. Moneymaker told me that if I didn't have a job by my next visit, she would have to violate my parole. I heard about a manager at Wendy's on Dickerson Road who hired felons and told her I planned to apply. The soonest interview was on the 17th, just four days before my next meeting with Moneymaker on the 21st. Not only did I have to get an interview but also walk away with proof of employment if I wanted to stay free.

The very next morning during my devotion, I heard a knock on the door. It was Don, a guy I knew from Mississippi. We talked for a while, then he said something that nearly knocked the wind out of me:

"I can get you a part-time job at a church, cleaning up."

"I sat back, amazed this was the confirmation from God I had been praying for during the last few months of my sentence."

"Yeah," he said with a smile.

Joy flooded through me. "If you get me on, I'll be the go-to man!"

Don laughed and called a man named Omar. He handed me his phone. Omar told me to come in for an interview the next morning at 10:00 a.m. I agreed. A few minutes later, Omar called back to give me the address, but I told him, "The Lord already showed me where it is." That's when it hit me the sign on Old Hickory Boulevard. The one the Spirit told me to remember, not the talk about pretty girls. God had been lining this up the whole time.

I went to the interview, and it felt like everything clicked. Omar seemed like he really wanted to hire me. I left full of hope, spiritually high, convinced this was God's plan unfolding. But a few days later, Don came back with disappointing news: the church didn't want to hire me after all because of my record.

The 17th finally came, and I showed up early for my 2:00 p.m. interview at Wendy's. The Holy Spirit nudged me to park on the drive-through side, so I did. I sat in the car, prayed, and tried to calm my nerves. At 1:45 p.m., just before walking inside, I heard someone call my name.

I turned and saw Omar from the church sitting in a car in the drive-through line. He asked what I was doing there. I told him I was about to head in for my interview. He paused for a moment and said, "Don't go in for that interview. You've got the job at the church. Just show up on Sunday and you can start." I hesitated, "Are you sure, bro? My P.O. is about to violate me if I don't bring back proof of a job." Omar looked me dead in the eye and said, "Yes, I'm sure."

Right then, I knew this wasn't just chance. That Wendy's interview time was really a divine appointment. If Omar hadn't gotten hungry at that exact moment, if the cashier had delayed him just a minute longer, or if my interview had been scheduled for 3:00 instead of 2:00, I would've missed him completely. But God lined it all up.

Soon after, Eboni and I agreed to work on our marriage. Within a year, we moved out of the projects into a brand-new three-bedroom home. That move was critical because I couldn't afford to be tied to the projects anymore one wrong step, and Moneymaker would send me back to prison. This new home gave us a real shot at a fresh start.

After prison, I hadn't seen much of Pops since getting out, but one night he called me crying, the first time I'd ever heard him cry. Life had gotten so hard that he'd been forced to move back to Mississippi before I came home, and he hated that. He asked me to pick him up so he could stay with me. I couldn't leave the state yet, so I told him to hold on until I cleared things with my P.O. But Pops couldn't wait. That same night, he called again, this time from the Nashville bus station. He was already there.

I picked him up and planned for him to stay at my baby's mama's old apartment in the projects. She kept the lease, and Pops covered the rent. That way, she'd always have somewhere to fall back on, and my kids finally got away from the bricks. But being out of the projects didn't solve everything. Eboni and the kids hated the new structure I was bringing into the house. Under my roof, we had rules: school and work on time every morning, dinner before 9:30 p.m., baths, and kids in bed by then. It was a whole new rhythm, and they weren't used to it. Arguments came often, and more than once, I found myself put out of the house.

On Sunday, I started working at Mount Zion Baptist Church in Nashville, TN, as a part-time member of the cleaning team. By Wednesday, I would need to report to Moneymaker, but that didn't bother me. God had already gone before me. I went from hearing Bishop Walker's voice through a prison radio to hearing him preach live and in person, just like I prayed for.

One of my main jobs in prison was maintaining the chapel, stripping, waxing, and buffing floors, so it felt like God had been training me all along. I always say, *God gives you practice before every blessing.* Before Moses freed the Israelites, he spent years tending sheep in the desert. Before David faced Goliath, he first faced lions and bears.

Years later, I realized that same principle applied to me. God was preparing me for this exact work, cleaning three church campuses: a 5,000-seat sanctuary with 28 bathrooms on Old Hickory Boulevard; a 1,750-seat campus with a plaza on Murfreesboro Road in Antioch; and the historic mother church on Jefferson Street, founded in 1866, with a 500-seat sanctuary and a basement full of bathrooms.

When Wednesday came, I was up early, dressed, and at the parole office before Moneymaker arrived. She looked at me and asked the question I'd been waiting for:
"Do you have proof of a job?" "Yes, ma'am," I said proudly. "I work for Mount Zion Baptist Church."

She called Omar to verify. After she hung up, she nodded. "You're good." Then she asked, "Can you pass a drug test?" I smiled and said, "Where's your cup?" She tried to keep a straight face but couldn't hide a small grin. "Bring proof of income within two to four weeks," she said. That was no problem.

Another unexpected blessing came through a familiar voice, Lonnie Greenlee, the man I once helped at the gas station when he said he needed four things: shoes, food, a last hit, and a ride to rehab. He called, saying he'd heard I was home and wanted to see me. When he pulled up, he was in a black Mercedes-Benz, dressed sharply like a businessman. He handed me some cash, and we went out to eat. That's when I learned he now owned several recovery houses and nearly half of East Nashville. God had truly turned his life around.

An Olive Branch Attempt

One day, I got a collect call it was Joe Ski. I hesitated for a second but accepted it. This was my chance to live out Matthew 5:44: *Love your enemies and pray for those who persecute you.*

Joe Ski's voice carried both surprise and hesitation, but what came next nearly floored me.
"What do I need to do to be saved?" he asked.

Right there over that prison phone, I walked him through the plan of salvation. As I spoke, a memory came flooding back—years ago, we were sitting on his mama's porch when she looked at us and said, "What y'all plan on doing in the near future?"

Without missing a beat, Joe Ski said, "We're going to start a church, and I'm gonna be the deacon."
She laughed a little and asked, "Who's gonna be the preacher?"
Joe Ski pointed at me and said, "He's standing right beside you."

Back then, I brushed it off. We had big dreams but small discipline the streets were still calling louder than God's voice. But now, standing on the other side of betrayal and redemption, I realized that moment wasn't just talk. It was prophecy.

This was one of those witnessing moments *the kind that reminded me I wasn't just surviving the trap, I was being transformed through it.*

. *When I hung up the phone that day, I sat in silence for a long time. The same man who once betrayed me, the one I never thought I could forgive, had just called me asking how to be saved. That moment showed me something powerful: this wasn't about me at all; it was all God's work.*

Only God could take a story like ours and turn it into a testimony. The same man who once helped cause me pain was now reaching out for prayer. The same streets that had divided us were now the backdrop of redemption. God was showing me firsthand what grace really looks like that forgiveness isn't weakness, it's obedience.

When Joe Ski asked how to be saved, I realized God had been preparing me all along. Every betrayal, every loss, every dark moment it was training for this. The trap wasn't just where I fell; it's where God began shaping my purpose. He used my pain to teach me how to speak to broken men, men like Joe Ski, in a way the world and sometimes even the church couldn't.

That call reminded me that you don't have to stand behind a pulpit to preach sometimes; your testimony is the sermon. Joe Ski's call was proof that even in your final moments, God can still use you as a witness, just like the thief on the cross. That thief didn't have time to live a new life, start a ministry, or right every wrong but in one conversation with Jesus, his soul was saved. Joe Ski's call reminded me that redemption doesn't need time; it just needs truth.

At the end of the call, I asked Joe Ski for his OCA number so I could bless him with some commissary. That didn't mean we were all good, but I knew forgiveness was part of my own healing. All that talk years ago about starting a church felt distant now my potential "Deacon Joe Ski" had joined the Crips in prison. It didn't surprise me when I later heard he'd gotten into it with some Bloods.

Through the prison ministry and connections at Mount Zion, I was able to make a few calls and get Joe Ski transferred to another facility for his safety. The warden who made the call attended Mount Zion himself it was God's hand all over again, turning pain into purpose.

Three years later, Joe Ski got released but only stayed free for seven months before being committed to a mental hospital. His caseworker called to tell me Joe Ski still looked up to me and asked if I would come visit him. The Middle Tennessee Mental Health Institute on Stewarts Ferry was just five minutes from my house, so I went.

When I saw him, Joe Ski was a shell of the man I used to know, zoned out, his words scattered. He said wild things about a twenty-year indictment and the Feds calling him to fly to the White House to pay taxes on the drugs he'd sold. His mind was gone, but before I left, I prayed that he would find peace the kind only God can give, the peace that surpasses all understanding.

Meanwhile, things at home weren't going well. My baby's mama wanted me out of the new house, so I moved in with Uncle Floyd. Before prison, I had covered 100% of the bills; now I could barely manage 50%. She was tired of hearing me say, "God will provide." Working at the church, I made just over $12,000 a year, the same amount I used to use for my *re-up* money every morning in the streets. Not long after I moved out, I heard rumors that a guy named Rock had moved into the house with my kids and their mother. I'd known Rock since we were young, never liked him much, but I respected him. Still, his reputation around the city was not good.

I Finally had a chance to pull up on Rock and told him straight up, "I don't care what you got going on with my baby's mama, but from the bottom of my heart, please don't put your hands on my kids." He said, "I can respect that. Matter of fact, I respect the change you've made. I never knew you were Red and J's daddy." Seven months later, she lost the house. Rock told her, "If you can't get along with your baby's daddy, you'll never get along with me, because that dude is 100." Not long after, he left her. So again, she was without. Every time she fell, I was right there to help her back up not because I still loved her, but because I believed all of us should be together under one roof.

No matter what was going on in my life, I went to work at the church every day with a smile on my face. Sometimes I'd work 17 hours straight, every day I could. When I had to take off, I'd still come in and work for free. To me, that was how I paid my tithes and offerings. The truth was, I was scared to be anywhere else so the church became my new block.

But just because you've given your life to Christ doesn't mean the devil stops trying to collect your soul. One day, out of nowhere, a spirit of suicide crept up on me. A dark thought whispered, *end it all.* Then, the Holy Spirit interrupted that thought:

"Do you remember that new CD player your mom wanted you to hook up in her room? Do you remember those damaged CDs the bookstore threw away, and how I told you to grab them? When you walk in, your brother E and his boys will be downstairs smoking and playing 2K but don't stop. Go upstairs to your mother's room. That CD player isn't for her, it's for this moment."

Just like He said, when I opened the door, E and his friends were smoking, and I stepped right over them. I found the boxes of CDs, reached in, and as soon as I touched one, I knew it was the one. I took it upstairs and pressed play. The sermon was *"Tell the Devil I Changed My Mind,"* by Bishop Joseph Walker. Within minutes, I was shouting, crying, and praising right there in my mama's room. God let me experience Psalm 107:20 all over again: *"He sent His word and healed them and delivered them from their destructions."*

That day I made a vow: *If I could serve the house of God as faithfully as I once served the trap houses, my life would truly change.* And it did. For the next ten years, I worked without missing a day no call-ins, no excuses. I was the first to show up and the last to leave, grinding for the kingdom like I once grinded for the streets.

The first paycheck stub I brought to Moneymaker was for only $385 for two weeks of work, but I was proud. The most I'd ever made in prison was $65 a month, so that stub felt like freedom in my hands. A few months later, Moneymaker called and told me I needed to have a full-time job 40 hours a week. For about five minutes, that bothered me. Then I remembered God's promise of favor over my life.

A month later, she called again but this time with a different tone. Her boss wanted to spotlight my story and feature it in the lobby of the probation office for other men to read. I asked about the full-time job requirement, and she said not to worry about it. That spotlight became my testimony. For a whole year, if you walked into the probation and parole office, you would see a display with my name, my picture, and my story. *That was all God.*

Not long after, Moneymaker called to say she'd be transferring my case to a lower level of parole. My new officer would be Erica Gomez. I didn't have to report in person anymore just call once a month. Truthfully, I didn't like it. I had started using my time at the parole office to minister to other guys waiting for their turn. I'd talk with them, pray with them, tell them what God had done for me. I did that until the Dickerson Pike office burned down in July of 2014.

Gomez and I got along fine until she noticed something I'd been giving her the same check stub for almost a year. One day, she called and said, "Larry Powell, if you don't get me an updated check stub down here ASAP, I'm putting a warrant out for your arrest after lunch." The truth was, I didn't know how to go online and print one off back then. It felt good to think I was getting over on the system… at least until that moment. I got her what she needed, and a year later, I was finally released from parole.

By then, I'd made up my mind this would be the last time my baby mama's chaos pulled me backward. I helped her get back on her feet again, and together we were blessed with a nice duplex in The Nations, West Nashville. But five months later, I was moving out again. She started coming home whenever she wanted. Some mornings, I'd already have the kids up and off to school before she'd pull up from wherever she'd been.

One weekend, she left for work Friday around 3 p.m. and didn't show up until 11 a.m. the next day. The moment she walked through the door, she said, "Stop calling my phone like a *****." I was done. I told my supervisor I had to leave work, went home, packed my things, and told her I wasn't coming back.

As I walked out the door, three-year-old Malia looked up and said, "Bye, Preacher." I froze. Those three small words hit me harder than any sermon ever could. It was like God Himself was speaking through her innocent voice, reminding me that His call on my life wasn't canceled just because things got hard. *That day, I realized my purpose wasn't behind me it was still unfolding ahead of me.*

Chapter 12:
The Trap Can't Hold Purpose Back

The Lord has made everything for his own purposes.
Proverbs 16:4

Freedom will test you long after the gates open. For me, the hardest traps weren't made of bars or bricks; they were emotional. Sometimes the lessons that shape you the most don't come from the streets or the system, but from the people you love. This chapter isn't just about heartbreak; it's about discernment about learning how misplaced loyalty and love can pull you back into bondage even after God has set you free.

Once again, I left my baby's mama with a nice roof over their head. Two weeks later, I saw her post on this new app called Facebook on a plane headed to Las Vegas with this old guy in a wheelchair. Four months later, she lost the duplex. I finally got the picture and learned this lesson: if you're living with your baby's mama, taking care of the home and paying her child support, that's a trap from hell. When she is upset and you guys fall out, she will have the card cut off.

I ended up moving in with my Uncle Floyd. He had a loft upstairs, a space he'd originally saved for my Uncle George, who was due home soon after serving a 20-year sentence in the penitentiary. Since I was already there, Uncle George and I would share the space once he got back.

Uncle Floyd never spoke badly about my baby's mama. He always told me, "When you get tired, that's when you'll do something different." That season finally came. Honestly, I didn't want to be separated from my kids or their mother. I always believed that if I fathered you, it's my job to protect and provide for everyone under one roof, especially with this woman. But child support was kicking my butt, and within a year, she lost two more homes without me there to help. One day, she called and asked if the boys could stay with me until she got back on her feet. I agreed but asked about the girls. She said she would keep them with her.

Separation, Divorce, And Birth Certificates

At 11 years old, Red asked me to make him a promise. He said his mom had some foolery going on and he wanted me to promise not to let anything happen to his sisters. I told him his sisters weren't my biological children, and there was only so much I could do but I'd do all I could. He understood that I loved Dajhia and Malia because they were his sisters.

Through those two girls, God gave me a revelation about forgiveness and redemption. With Dajhia, I learned the true power of forgiveness. It's something sacred when you can honestly forgive both people who betrayed you just like Jesus forgave Judas. That's where I believe most of my spiritual growth came from. I've learned over the years to give God glory for every situation that pulls you closer to Him. After all, we are all adopted into God's family as His chosen children (Ephesians 1:5).

Eboni my baby's mama did something different when she filled out Malia's birth certificate. On Dajhia's certificate, she listed her last name as Ridley, not Powell. But when she filled out Malia's, she marked that she was married, which meant by law, the baby's last name had to be *Powell.*

The Department of Health caught the error when they saw the inconsistency. Eboni tried to explain, "Larry was in prison it's no way he's the father." But legally, because we were still married, the last name had to remain Powell. To correct it, she had to change Malia's certificate to match. So, Malia became a Powell. And even in child support court, the judge said, "Whatever one party does wrong during a marriage, the other party is just as responsible." That's how I ended up paying child support for Malia too. In that moment, I understood something deeper: God really is married to the backslider. Even when we make mistakes, He still claims us as His own.

Life was going good so far. One afternoon, I noticed a news van parked outside my house. When I stepped out to see what was going on, the reporter told me they'd spotted my van with the *Hustlers Anonymous* signs on both sides parked at a store in the hood and wanted to know more about my ministry. At first, I laughed and asked if they had the right person. They explained they were doing a story about my life and how I started *Hustlers Anonymous*. I agreed, and the producer asked me to bring two guys I'd been mentoring to the interview.

I called Fat Boy first, but finding the second person proved harder until the Holy Spirit told me, *"Call Lil' David."* When I did, he showed up immediately. Two hours after the news crew left, the Spirit reminded me of something I told Lil' David years ago while we were locked up: *"One day, we'll be explaining this kind of preaching to the news."* That's why it was so hard to find anyone else God had already written this moment. He wanted Lil' David to be part of it, to strengthen his faith and remind him that the Word always comes full circle.

By this time, I was working full-time at the church. God's favor was showing up everywhere I had a work cell phone, a church email, and even access to drive the ministry's vehicles. They gave me access to a pearl white Yukon Denali to handle church business, the same Denali that transported Bishop Walker from one Mt. Zion location to the next Mt. Zion location. Folks in the streets thought it was mine. Next thing I know, rumors started flying that I was back selling dope. One old street dude even tried to sell me some guns with blue-tip bullets. I told him straight up, "You got the wrong man, bro."

The truth was, my personal car was a beat-up Acura with a green bungee cord holding the hood down so it wouldn't fly up on the interstate. That car smoked so bad after church that I had to wait for the parking lot to clear because it would smoke out all the cars behind me! Still, I was grateful I was working for the Kingdom now, and that came with more blessings than I could count.

When they handed me my first church phone, I prayed, *"Lord, let this phone ring just as much as my old crack phone."* And He delivered because that phone never stopped ringing! Members called about lost items, vendors checked in, and the church stayed busy. Even during the pandemic, when the world slowed down, God's work didn't. Just like He promised, *there's never a drought when it comes to His work.* My church phone rang twice as much as my trap phone ever did. The Mount always had events going on, which kept me off the streets.

Shortly after I started working full-time, I was blessed to lease a beautiful brick home sitting on an acre and a half of land. Back in 2005 three years before I ever walked out of the penitentiary God asked me the same question, He once asked King Solomon: *"What do you want from Me?"* Without hesitation, I told Him, "Lord, I want to be a pastor Nashville has never seen before. Help me win platinum souls for Your Kingdom, just like You let Young Buck go platinum in music."

Looking back on that moment now brings tears to my eyes. I can see how God's hand guided me through every struggle, every test, every setback turning broken places into blessings. I remember when an ice storm hit one winter, and I got a call asking if I would open the church doors in such bad weather. I said to myself, *"If I opened the crack house doors in weather like this, then I'll sure open the Lord's House."* As facility manager, it was my job to be the first one in and the last one out, and I carried that responsibility like ministry.

In 2011, I finally filed for divorce from my baby's mama. My lawyer spent most of her time in juvenile court trying to get Malia taken off my child support case. The thought of fighting for custody had never crossed my mind until one day she asked me, "Do you want custody of your boys?" When I said yes, she changed the hearing date to give me time to prepare.

Child support was still hitting hard. By then, Red and J were 10 and 11, living full-time with me, but their mama still had the child support card. Our next court date came, and the judge ruled in my favor he took me off child support that same day and ordered her to pay me back for the months she'd been using the money, even though the boys lived with me. When she filed taxes, the refund came straight to me.

Red and J didn't like that. It showed on their faces every morning when I used my child support card for gas to take them to the bus stop. It wasn't about money; it was about perspective. No matter how much a child's mother might struggle, most kids will still stand by her. I understood that. It takes both parents to make a family work, but in a child's heart, mama is golden.

By this point, Red and J had been with me for two and a half years. Three males under one roof meant a lot of testosterones and a lot of lessons. I taught them to do laundry, clean the kitchen, and take responsibility for their space. But there were things a father couldn't replace a mother's tenderness, her nurture, her presence. The absence of that created scars I could see but couldn't always heal. Spiritually, mentally, and emotionally, they were hurting. The hardest part was watching them carry resentment toward me for taking them away from their mother without realizing she was battling addiction and couldn't provide for them. I had to love them through their misunderstanding and let time reveal the truth.

By the time the kids got older, pieces of the past started to make sense. One night after a 17-hour shift at the church, I came in to find Red asleep in my bed, his sisters curled up beside him, and their mother passed out on the couch. The house looked like it had been patched together for a moment of peace.

"Red, what's going on?" I asked.

"I'm just making sure Mom and the girls are good," he said without opening his eyes.

I remembered the promise I made years ago about protecting his sisters. "Son," I said, "I told you I'd do my part, but your mom ain't my whole responsibility anymore."

"She just needs to rest and get a fresh start for the morning," Red answered.

"Alright," I said. "Give me my bed back and go sleep on the couch with her. You're lucky I ain't got a woman in my life right now, this would be a different story." Three weeks later, Red had them back under that roof again. He never trusted the men his mother dated after our divorce. He taught Dajhia and Malia to run across the street for help if their mother's boyfriend ever put his hands on their mother again. I later learned his warning wasn't empty one of those men shot her in the leg.

We tried to keep our fights from becoming family wars, but anger has a way of showing up at the worst time. At a family gathering in Mound Bayou, Mississippi, I asked Red to move his phone so I could charge mine. Thirty minutes passed, and my phone still wasn't on the charger. I threw a football at his chest, a stupid, childish thing to do, and he jumped up like a cornered man. I stood up, ready to discipline him. Before I could hit him, our cousins pulled us apart and tried to hold me back. Red took advantage, walked over, and hit me five times, while my cousins were holding my hands behind my back. My face swelled in a way it never had before. That night, the silence after the fight made me see it all clearer: the cost of the life I led, the damage passed down to my boys, and how the very thing I tried to protect them from had crept inside our home.

Honestly, I wanted to kill Red and leave him in the red dirt of the Mississippi streets. For a second there, the rage took over every worst-case scenario ran through my head, but my family begged me not to do something I'd regret. I didn't want Kettle kicked out of her place because of us fighting. Red still had to ride back to Nashville with me, so I forced myself to hold it together.

The drive back was silent and heavy. When we got home, the anger was still raw. J was with us and could feel it. I pulled Red into the basement and made him touch everything in sight. I wasn't beating him to break him, but I wanted him to feel the weight of discipline; I manhandled him hard enough to make a point, slamming him against boxes and the washer until he stumbled free and ran to his room. I told him you don't fight your father. I was loud, angry, and scared all at once because part of me also feared he might reach for a gun.

After that night, Red went back to his mom's, and J stayed with me. Two days later, Red returned to school with visible bruises. When asked about them, he told the school counselor he had gotten into a fight with another kid at the community center. That situation gave us room to breathe and for J and me to start rebuilding trust. J began to see that my push was about boundaries and protection. Six weeks later, Red moved back in. Living with the instability at his mom's, with lights cut, fights, and chaos, helped him see the difference, and a month after that, I did a cell search of his room. I found contraband and cash that could have gotten us evicted or me sent back inside. My first impulse was to lash out, but I'd learned to play chess, not checkers. I left the items in place and set new rules: I would do room checks at 3 a.m., and when I said, "report to the living room," I meant it. No arguing. If you have anything illegal, remove it now or face the consequences. After that shakedown, I never found contraband again.

On Red's 18th birthday, he moved into a beautiful condo in Bellevue and convinced his mom to let his sisters live with him. The condo had three levels, and one of them had a master suite just for the girls. Red's biggest "turn up" in life wasn't designer clothes, shoes, or jewelry though he had all those things it was turning up for his family. Providing for them made him feel whole, like he was finally being the man he'd always wanted to be.

But the trap has a way of disguising itself as love and loyalty. Red had started selling weed at 14, using his phone to move product, and he kept that hustle going until his adult age. Proverbs 19:18 says, "Discipline your son, for in that there is hope; do not be a willing party to his death." That verse hits differently when you've been through pain and struggle.

No matter where you go in this world, there's a painful truth that follows us: young Black men are killing other young Black men and going to prison at an alarming rate. A study showed that 14% of people who grew up in North Nashville in the early 1980s were incarcerated by their 30s (WZTV). Those men became the parents of the children born in the 2000s, the generation now that's fighting the same cycle.

The ACE (Adverse Childhood Experiences) study documented how trauma before age 18 can shape a person's future. It revealed that the more trauma a child endures, the greater the risk of addiction, mental illness, and destructive behavior later in life. Children in the welfare system often experience four or more ACEs before adulthood.

Eboni and I being incarcerated at the same time was one of those ACEs for our kids. Our choices became their weight to carry. J once told me how angry he was when his mom gave Red her entire $7,500 child support back pay from Joe Ski, trusting him to "flip it" by selling drugs. That money and that moment became another ACE. When the Bible says to discipline your son, it doesn't mean punishment; it means teaching him how to measure his steps. It means setting boundaries, explaining consequences, and modeling what it looks like to walk in wisdom. Without that, the world will discipline them in its own way, and its lessons come with blood and time.

One Sunday afternoon at Greater Covenant Church, a small outreach church on the east side, I'd visited before I met Jessica Ward. She was on the hospitality team: always smiling, always moving, always making space for people. Her generosity and quiet service hit me in a way nothing else had. I'd always been honest about my past; some girls like the bad-boy image, but by then I'd shed that life, and I was looking for something different. We started dating in 2014 and got married in 2019. Meeting her was the kind of small mercy that turns into a whole new season.

Not long after, I was invited to speak in a Metro-sponsored drug-prevention program for middle-school kids. While a retired soldier was giving his testimony, an eleven-year-old raised his hand and asked, with dead quiet in the room, "How many bodies do you have under your belt?" That question landed in my chest like a stone. It wasn't curiosity, it was a wounded, trained expectation of violence. That moment reminded me how deep the damage runs. That kid had already been given an ACE before he could even spell it out.

Proverbs 19:18 says, "Discipline your son, for in that there is hope; do not be a willing party to his death." That verse has stuck with me. The last line is the hard part: do not be a willing party to his death. Death here isn't only bullets or blood. Life ruined by prison, addiction, or wasted potential that's a kind of death, too. If we let our kids grow up inside a culture that teaches them how to aim before it teaches them how to read, if we fill their heads with guns-on-repeat and leave their hearts empty of structure and love, then we are partners in the outcome.

So, what do we do? We discipline with love. Discipline means boundaries, consequences, teaching responsibility, and holding steady when it's easier to look away. It means reading scripture with them instead of leaving them alone to play Call of Duty and expecting a miracle. It means teaching trades and skills alongside truth, showing how dignity and work walk together. It means being the first one up and the last one home. It means modeling faith when your hands shake.

Most importantly, it means hope is not a naive wish; it's a posture and a practice. I started Hustlers Anonymous inside the prison for that reason: to give men a twelve-step map that met their language, their hunger, and their pain. I learned to preach with the street in my bones and the Gospel in my mouth. I saw men change. I watched sons come back from the brink. I watched a neighborhood breathe a little easier when somebody decided to show up, again and again.

We can't erase every scar from the past, but we can refuse to hand those scars down like a family heirloom. We can stop being willing partners in the fast deaths around us. We can teach, protect, and model a different story, a story that says, through discipline and mercy, there is hope.

Chapter 13:
"Trapped but Still Chosen."

I've held bricks, I've held bars, and I've held my own kids in a casket. But the heaviest thing I ever held was my faith and I ain't letting go.
Dr. Larry Powell.

There comes a point in every journey when the fight moves from the streets to the soul. For me, this chapter is that turning point the moment when faith and pain collided. The same man who once hustled for survival now serves while wounded, carrying scars that became testimonies. What follows is not just a story of loss it's a story of how even through tragedy, God still calls, still covers, and still uses us for His glory.

In 2014, I enrolled at Emmanuel Bible College in Nashville. Over the course of six and a half years, I earned my Bachelor's, Master's, and Doctor of Ministry (D.Min.) degrees a journey that required equal parts faith, focus, and endurance. During that time, I worked a full-time job, attended school full time, and preached at the county jail. My schedule was relentless, but it was fueled by a purpose greater than exhaustion.

I also volunteered as a preacher and teacher within the Tennessee prison system, the Tennessee juvenile system, and various drug-court programs. I served as a board member and spiritual leader for Still Standin Foundation, a nonprofit founded by Zay Maxwell, and as a mentor for 4:13 Strong, a program rooted in Philippians 4:13 "I can do all things through Christ who strengthens me." Through that work, I guided young men, ages 18 to 30, teaching them that the same energy they once used to destroy their lives could be redirected to build something greater.

But even while I was out helping others, my greatest test was waiting for me at home. One may wonder how I could balance all this and still be a full-time single parent. That's where my relationship with my son, J, took a turn for the worse.

One evening, J was sitting in his car smoking weed in an unfamiliar community. Someone called the police. When they arrived, they found J high as a kite, with no driver's license, and extra weed in the backseat. One of the officers recognized my last name and wondered if J was my son. Once J confirmed his full name, the officer called me directly. He said he'd hold J at the location until I arrived and even offered not to tow the car if I could get someone to drive it home.

I thanked him and hung up the phone. On my way there, I wasn't just a preacher or a mentor I was a father walking into a test that would challenge everything I'd learned about grace, patience, and faith. As I drove, the realization hit me hard my son was now walking through the same struggles I had once lived myself. There's a mix of pain and understanding in that moment. It hurts because I could see what was coming before he even did. It felt like watching my past trying to pull him into the same trap I had escaped.

When I pulled up to that scene, anger wrestled with compassion inside of me. On the surface, I was frustrated disappointed to see him caught in the very cycle I had warned him about. But beneath that anger was a father's concern, a deep ache that only comes from wanting to protect your child from the same pain you once endured.

As I looked at my son, standing there lost between youth and manhood, I realized that God was testing my leadership not from the pulpit, but from the pain. In that moment, I understood that fatherhood isn't about control; it's about covering. Could I lead with love when my heart was breaking? Could I correct him without crushing him? These were the questions I carried silently as I walked toward him, determined to lead my son the way God had led me with grace, truth, and mercy.

On the way home, J and I had a talk that would change our relationship forever. I asked him what he had learned from everything that had just happened. Without hesitation, he said, "I can't believe the police called you. I thought you were working with them." His words hit hard. My own son thought I was siding with the same system that once locked me up. He didn't realize that my relationship with law enforcement had changed because I had changed. Over the years, many officers had come to trust me not as a criminal but as a man of God who could help bring peace to tense situations instead of chaos.

I took a deep breath before answering him. "Son," I said, "you've been right beside me when my mentees, guys your age, were caught with a gun or caught up in the system. You've seen how the police will sometimes call me before they take them downtown. You've seen how God has given me favor with people in high places."

It hurt to know that my son, the one who had witnessed my transformation, now doubted my loyalty to him. That accusation cut deep not just as a preacher, but as a father who's lived on both sides of the system. Hearing J say those words made me feel misunderstood, disrespected, and heartbroken. It's one thing to be judged by the world, but it's another when the judgment comes from your own child.

Still, I realized that my role in that moment wasn't to defend my name it was to protect his soul. God was testing me, not through the pulpit, but through pain. This moment challenged me as both a father and a faith leader. It tested my ability to lead even when I felt disrespected, to love even when I was being misunderstood. As the tension hung in the air, I reminded myself that fatherhood reflects ministry. It's not about proving who you are it's about staying grounded in who God called you to be. I stopped asking, "Why me?" and started saying, "Use me."

It also reminded me of something deeper the distance that sometimes forms between a father and a son when one tries to walk away from the life the other is just beginning to understand. I thought back to a similar moment with one of my mentees, JO.

JO had called me from prison, furious and confused. He'd been locked up for ten years on a nonviolent drug charge and had finally gone up for parole. I had spoken at his hearing myself. He completed every requirement the board demanded, so he could be released. But one morning, they transferred him to another prison for a program called TCOM a therapeutic community program for inmates with drug-related offenses or addictions. I remember listening to his voice over that prison phone, his frustration breaking through the static. He couldn't understand why God would let him come that close to freedom only to send him backward. As I listened, I saw myself in him and now, I saw both of us in my son. The same confusion, the same frustration, the same struggle between faith and circumstance. Faith doesn't always move the mountain; sometimes it strengthens you to climb it.

However, when JO went up for parole again, the board did not release him. Their report showed that he hadn't completed the recommended program. The truth was, he had completed it the only issue was that the program had a different name at the new prison.

The parole board didn't care to hear the explanation, nor did the staff or caseworkers want to advocate for him. They warned JO to stop arguing or risk being written up for insubordination a move that would have damaged his record even further. I told JO to calm down and call me back later. Then, I picked up my phone and made a call downtown to one of my friends in high places. After explaining the situation, he told me he'd look into it and would call back by the end of the week. Before he could, JO called again, excitement bursting through his voice. "Boy, I don't know who you know," he said, "but these people came in here apologizing to me and everything! I got an out date for a halfway house. Whoever you know got the juice! "I laughed and told him, "I know God, homie. And the juice is the blood of Christ."

Later, I gave J another example to help him understand the kind of influence God had given me. A guy I had mentored for years everyone knew him as *Slick* called from the West Coast asking for prayer after being locked up again. J knew him as a neighborhood superstar, but I knew him as a young man who'd been bound over to adult jail on his 18th birthday.

No matter how much fame or street respect Slick had earned, he never lost his respect for me. He had witnessed firsthand how the Lord lifted

me from the streets and molded me into who I had become. So, I asked J a question that still echoes in my spirit:
"How is it that I can be trusted on the streets and in the prison system but not in my own household?"

Even with the examples I gave, J couldn't comprehend the level of favor and influence God had allowed me to walk in. His perception was clouded by a spiritual battle much deeper than either of us could see at that moment. The same spirit that had chased me in my youth, the spirit of Balaam, which loves the profit of unrighteousness, was now attacking my son. It had come through the music, the culture, the very streets we once walked. The same voice that once told me to be 2Pac was whispering to J to be Young Dolph. It had him chasing pride, validation, and identity in all the wrong places.

But I recognized it immediately because I had already fought that spirit myself. The difference now was that another spirit had attached itself to J paranoia. He began to believe that everyone was against him, including me, his family, and even the doctors trying to help.

He started showing signs of mental distress, wearing coats in the heat, speaking words that didn't make sense, his thoughts tangled in fear and confusion. Doctors tried to run tests, but J resisted. He didn't want a CAT scan of his brain because he believed the machine could read his thoughts. In his mind, they were trying to get information about the streets from him.

That's when I knew my son wasn't just battling addiction or rebellion, he was fighting a spiritual war for his mind. There were moments I didn't know how to hold it all together. Watching my son's mental health decline while still leading others took a toll on me. I had to learn that sometimes the preacher in me needed to sit down so the father in me could stand up. I didn't need to quote scripture in those moments; I needed to be present. I needed to hold him, pray silently, and trust that God could reach him where my words could not and in those quiet nights, when the weight of my calling pressed against the grief of my family, I wrestled with a truth I rarely spoke out loud: I could use my influence to set other men free but still struggled to reach my own sons. That kind of pain doesn't make headlines. It's the kind you smile through in public and pray about in private.

The Breaking Point

This spirit is exceptionally strong. It attacks young men who are lost those searching for purpose in all the wrong places. It offers a false sense of identity through the streets and convinces them that destruction is success. I told J the truth that day: the only way to defeat that spirit is through prayer and fasting, by staying grounded in the Word of God, and leaning on the power of the Holy Spirit. Through counseling sessions with J, I began to learn more about the hidden trauma the ACEs (Adverse Childhood Experiences) that shaped his behavior and mindset. Things I never knew about came to the surface.

He told me about the time he saw someone he knew get shot right in front of him and had to duck behind a car. He told me about the day the drug unit kicked in his mama's door looking for Rock, one of her boyfriends. These were moments that no child should have to experience, moments that shaped the pain he carried in silence.

He also admitted that when I came home from prison, he didn't know how to receive me. Red always knew me as "Daddy." But to J, I was just another stranger in and out of his mother's life, another man who had once lived the same street life he was now surrounded by. That realization broke me. My absence had cost him his trust.

I prayed constantly for my son.
"Lord, please heal J's mind, his heart, his spirit."
And I would always end with the same plea:
Keep J in your prayers.

Then, life delivered a blow I could never have prepared for.

On my 45th birthday in 2022, I woke up to what would become the worst day of my life. I rolled over, grabbed my phone, and saw a text from Red. It read:

“Happy birthday, Pops. I didn’t want to tell you this, but she’s gone, Daddy. She’s gone. Malia got killed last night.”

My heart dropped. I could feel his pain through the text. My hands shook as I tried to call him no answer. I searched Malia’s name online, hoping it was a mistake. But there it was in bold letters:

A 14-year-old was stabbed to death at a bus stop outside a Walmart parking lot in Nashville, Tennessee.

The report said a fight broke out between two groups of girls. One of the girls, just sixteen years old, charged at Malia with a pocketknife. She stabbed my daughter nine times!

Metro Police confirmed that Malia Powell had been transported to the hospital, where she was later pronounced dead. Her killer, Isabella Jocson, was charged with criminal homicide.

Malia was just fourteen vibrant, full of joy, a cheerleader at Bellevue Middle School. She was loved by everyone who knew her. Her laughter had a way of lighting up an entire room. Losing her was like losing light itself.

Her death shattered our family. It tore something from Red that never healed.

Nine weeks after Malia’s funeral, I was driving home from a Mt. Zion church picnic when my phone rang. It was Eboni, her voice trembling.

“Someone just shot and killed Red,” she said.

The words hit me harder than any punch, harder than any prison sentence. My body went numb. I tried calling his phone. No answer. I called my wife, Jessica, and told her to be ready when I got there. I was heading to the scene. My son was gone.

I drove as fast as I could to the North side. The moment I saw the yellow tape surrounding Red's car, I knew the truth. A homicide detective I knew met me at the scene and confirmed what my spirit already felt: Red was gone.

I wanted to run under that tape and hold him one last time. I wanted to tell him I was proud of him, that I loved him, that he could rest now. But the police wouldn't let me near him.

In that moment, I thought about the irony of his life, how he came into this world breaking free from an amniotic bag, and now he was leaving it zipped in a body bag. That image never leaves me. It's the kind of pain no father should ever have to endure.

When I think back on that season, I didn't process it all at once I survived in pieces. Emotionally, I was torn between anger and numbness. Mentally, I battled memories that wouldn't let me rest. Physically, grief sat on me like a body I couldn't lift.

In the days and nights that followed, my conversations with God weren't polished prayers they were raw cries. Some nights I said nothing. He didn't give me an answer; He gave me Himself. If I could speak to another father or mother still praying for their children, even when it feels too late or too painful, I'd tell them this: *Don't stop praying.* You may not see change yet, but your prayers are seeds that God waters in His time. Even if your child is gone, God can still use your story to save somebody else's child.

When Hope Fulfills

The next day, the news reported that a 19-year-old faced a criminal warrant in the Saturday night shooting death of a 22-year-old man, my son. Authorities said the suspect had also been wounded by return gunfire.

By Sunday, Metro Police had issued a criminal homicide warrant for Treyvon Palmer, 19, who was receiving treatment at Nashville General

Hospital for a gunshot wound. Treyvon had tried to rob Red for a necklace that read *"Da Real RED."*

He was armed with a pistol that had an auto sear, which the streets call a *Glock switch*, a small, illegal device that turns a handgun into a machine gun. That's an enormous amount of firepower for young, untrained men to be playing with in the broken streets of America.

The report from Nashville.gov read:

September 11, 2022: A criminal homicide warrant has been obtained for 19-year-old Treyvon Palmer for Saturday evening's fatal shooting of 22-year-old Jawauntez Powell inside the Corner Mart at 2600 Clarksville Pike. The investigation, led by Detective Timothy Skopek, indicates the two were in line with merchandise when Palmer suddenly made physical contact with Powell. Palmer pointed a firearm at Powell. Powell pulled his own gun and fired at Palmer, apparently in self-defense. Palmer then fired multiple shots at Powell. Powell died at the scene.

The shock of losing my firstborn in such a careless, violent way is indescribable. I had already buried one child, and now I stood at the edge of another grave, trying to hold on to my sanity, but even in that darkness, God allowed one small ray of light to break through: two weeks before Red died, he gave his life to Christ. That was my hope, the same hope I spoke of earlier from Proverbs 19:18. The hope that this generation of young men and women, born in the 2000s, might come to know Christ before the streets claimed them.

It's a strange kind of peace the kind that only grace can explain. The same streets that tried to claim me had claimed my son, but before they did, God had already claimed his soul. That's the hope I hold on to the hope that love and redemption don't die with the body.

Red left behind a beautiful little girl, Paris Andrea Powell. Red and I had always wanted a boy, but when we laid eyes on her, we forgot all about it. She looked just like her daddy, my mama, and me. Every time I see her, I see pieces of Red smiling back at me a reminder that legacy can outlive loss.

But grief has a way of multiplying. Just as our family began to process Red's death, my mama texted me: "The ambulance just rushed Pops to the hospital. It doesn't look good. I hate to tell you this right now." Before I could even make it there, she called again and said the words no son wants to hear:

"He's gone."

Before the autopsy report on Malia could come back, we had to start one for Red.
Before Red's report returned, we had to begin one for my daddy.
Before the dirt on Malia's grave could settle, we had to dig Red's.
Before the dirt on Red's grave could harden, we had to dig another for my daddy.
Before we could close the deal on Malia's headstone, we had to choose Red's. We decided on a double stone side by side.
Before that deal could be completed, we had to choose one more for my father.

And through all of it, I gave thanks to the Kingdom of God. Because even in pain, He was still present. There were moments I'd sit in silence and ask, *"Lord, how much more can one heart handle?"* I heard a whisper back: "All things work together for good." That verse became my anchor in the storm. I had to live through pain that didn't feel good before I could understand how God could use it for good. What once felt like loss became the very thing He used to teach me endurance, empathy, and unshakable faith.

I never thought in a million years I would be the one preaching both my son's and my father's funerals within two weeks of each other. I had spoken words of comfort at Malia's funeral just weeks before laying her brother to rest. My first committal service was for my son, and my second for my daddy. I never wanted to preach those sermons, but I came to understand they were part of my assignment, an unthinkable calling that only God could have prepared me for.

So, when you see me wearing the *Big Homie* clothing line when you see *"God Is My Big Homie"* across my chest please understand it hits different for me. Because death is Big Homie's call. When I look back over my life, I can see that even through grief, God was preparing me. Even in my prison cell, He was equipping me for the pain I would one day endure and for the purpose that would follow it.

His Word never fails:

"And we know that all things work together for good to those who love God, to those who are called according to His purpose."
—Romans 8:28

When Faith Has to Stand Alone

Still, at this point, I began to question God.
"Lord," I said, "did You call me into ministry just to preach my family's funerals?"

As those words left my mouth, another devastating call came my uncle, George Gordon, had passed away of natural causes. Once again, I found myself preparing to preach another funeral my third committal service for yet another family member.

And yet, even as I stood over another casket, I whispered, *"Thank You, Lord."*

What does it mean to give thanks to the Kingdom while enduring so much loss?
That's where faith grows up. Giving thanks in loss doesn't mean you're okay with what happened it means you still trust who God is.

I wish I could say my story ends there but it doesn't.

Around February 2024, on a Monday, Eboni, my children's mother, called with a trembling voice. She said J hadn't come home, and she was getting worried. She tried to file a missing person's report, but the police couldn't take it until seventy-two hours had passed. They told her to wait, maybe he'd show back up.

Tuesday came, and still no word from J. Eboni called again. "It's been seventy-two hours," she said, "but today is Malia's birthday. I just don't have the energy to fill out a report for another missing child."

We agreed to wait one more day.

But before I could make it back home, my phone rang again. This time, her voice broke completely:

"He's dead. He's dead!"

J had walked seven blocks from her house and shot himself in the face. He died instantly.

My heart must have fallen out of my chest. I could barely breathe.

At the time, I was still recovering from surgery. Just a week before, a CAT scan had revealed a small lump no bigger than a pea on my thyroid. The doctors said it was a fifty-fifty chance it could be cancer. Three specialists later, they still couldn't confirm, so they strongly advised surgery. I had my thyroid removed, and before I could even heal, I was facing the unthinkable again.

Three of my children are gone within eighteen months. Eboni wanted J buried beside his brother and sister. I agreed. When I went to the cemetery, I asked if there was a slot near them available, and it was. The next day at the funeral home, we planned another service. And once again, I had to do what no father should ever have to do: I preached my own son's funeral.

What did I feel standing in the pulpit again, delivering my own child's eulogy for the third time?

It felt like my heart and my calling were fighting for the same space. The pulpit that once felt like power now felt like a cross.

Even through all of this, through the exhaustion, the confusion, the raw grief I kept serving. I kept preaching in prisons, standing before young men who were out here killing, while knowing that another young man had killed my son. I kept speaking against suicide while mourning the suicide of my own child. I continued advocating for juveniles not to be sentenced to life in prison, even though the young woman who killed my daughter was serving time. I kept ministering through my own pain because that's what God called me to do. There were moments when the pulpit became my battlefield, and the sermon became my lifeline. I preached one message during that season that hit differently than any other:

Mark 9:14-21 "Bring the boy to Me."

All three of my children's funerals were as beautiful as something like that could ever be. But each one left a scar that only heaven can heal. Mental illness is at an all-time high in this country. We must stand together, as one community, to fight this invisible war.

Today, J rests beside his brother and sister, three souls together again:
Malia in Plot 9.
Jawauntez, "Red," in Plot 10.
Jacquell, "J," in Plot 11.

I've already started looking into whether their double headstone can become a triple. Every time I visit their graves, tears fill my eyes—not only for my children, but for all the other young souls buried there. So many names carved in stone, so many born in the 2000s.

Still… I pray.

One day, I stopped by my mother's house to drop off some groceries. As she unpacked the bags, I stood quietly, watching her hands move with grace and patience. In that moment, it hit me: I was looking at a woman who, within just 18 months, had buried her husband of 37 years and three of her grandchildren. Yet, somehow, she still stood strong. She still smiled. She still found ways to live to find joy and purpose again. She spends her time now visiting family in Mississippi, cherishing the grandchildren she has left, and staying connected to life.

Maybe it was all the pain our family had endured the deaths of my children, the weight of generational struggle that moved my brother E to change course. He finally stepped away from the streets and found steady, legal work. Now he's raising three beautiful children: Eric Powell, Erinikco Powell (a combination of his and Nicole's names), and Kendrick Powell, who carries my middle name. E and I still reflect often on how far we've come the roads we traveled, the temptations we survived, and the grace that carried us both. We know the life we lived could've ended a thousand different ways, but instead, it grew us.

Like my mother, Eboni continues to carry the unthinkable grief of losing three children. She finds strength through her daughter Dajhia, who graduated high school and is now studying cosmetology a living reminder that beauty can still rise from broken places. Joe Ski, on the other hand, is still fighting his battles with mental health. He lives in his mother's house, trying to stay grounded. I check on him from time to time. Sometimes he tries to connect, other times he pulls away. I understand his patterns now and try to love him where he is. He has seven children, and they do their best to support him. *I pray for him often.* My only grandchild, Paris, Red's daughter, lives with her mother. I see her as often as I can. She carries her father's light in her smile, and seeing her reminds me that even in loss, legacy lives on.

HUSTLERS ANONYMOUS

Selling drugs is an addiction just like using them. When I went to prison, I realized that most of the men behind bars weren't monsters; they were survivors. Most were nonviolent offenders caught in the trap of trying to feed their families the only way they knew how. Today's streets are different. Fentanyl has turned the hustle deadly. Crack might have ruined lives, but fentanyl ends them. In prison, I noticed something else. There were programs to help users, but nothing for the sellers. Nobody seemed to understand that the *high* of a hustler wasn't the drug, it was the deal.

The rush of making a sale, flipping a profit, and feeding your family. That kind of intoxication needed its own kind of recovery. So, I prayed and asked God to show me how to heal that mindset. He gave me twelve spiritual steps the steps that would later become *Hustler's Anonymous*. I worked those steps like a man fighting for his own freedom, and little by little, they worked. God took the same discipline I once used to destroy my life and turned it into discipline to rebuild others. He turned my addiction to the streets into a calling to serve the lost.

Hustlers Anonymous (H.A.)

- **Step 1.** We admit that we are addicted to selling drugs. Only God has the power to deliver us. *"There is a way that seems right to a man, but its end is the way of death."* (Proverbs 14:12)
- **Step 2.** We believe that God, through Jesus, can renew our minds. *"For God did not send his Son into the world to judge the world, but that the world should be saved through Him."* (John 3:17)
- **Step 3.** We decide to turn our lives over to God through Jesus. *"I urge you, therefore, brethren, by the mercies of God, to present your bodies a living and holy sacrifice, acceptable to God, which is your spiritual service of worship."* (Romans 12:1)

- **Step 4.** We examine ourselves and take an honest inventory. *"Let us examine and probe our ways and let us return to the Lord."* (Lamentations 3:40)
- **Step 5.** We confess our sins to God and to another person. *"Therefore, confess your sins to one another and pray for one another, so that you may be healed."* (James 5:16)
- **Step 6.** We desire a new way of life. *"Delight yourself in the Lord, and He will give you the desires of your heart."* (Psalm 37:4)
- **Step 7.** We ask God to reveal His purpose for our lives. *"For by Him were all things created… all things were created by Him and for Him."* (Colossians 1:16)
- **Step 8.** We forgive those who have hurt us, and we ask forgiveness from those we've harmed. *"Just as you want people to treat you, treat them in the same way."* (Luke 6:31)
- **Step 9.** We comfort others as God has comforted us. *"Who comforts us in all our tribulation, that we may be able to comfort those who are in any trouble, with the comfort with which we ourselves are comforted of God."* (2 Corinthians 1:4)
- **Step 10.** We put Christ first in everything. *"Trust in the Lord with all your heart, and do not lean on your own understanding. In all your ways acknowledge Him, and He will make your paths straight."* (Proverbs 3:5-6)
- **Step 11.** We study and meditate on God's Word daily. *"But seek first His kingdom and His righteousness, and all these things shall be added to you."* (Matthew 6:33)
- **Step 12.** Now awakened to righteousness, we carry Christ's message to others. *"Go home to your people and report to them what great things the Lord has done for you, and how He had mercy on you."* (Mark 5:19)

A LIFE REDEEMED

Today, I live my life with gratitude, not pride, in every choice I make, but deep thankfulness for every lesson I learned along the way. Even in my darkest seasons, God never stopped valuing me. He never stopped calling me.

Through His grace, I now serve as a board member and spiritual leader for several life-changing organizations that give back to the same streets I once took from:

- **4:13 Strong** – Empowering young men ages 18 to 30 to build their faith, character, and future through discipline, hard work, and the Word of God.
- **Still Standin Foundation** – A movement helping individuals rise from trauma and transition into triumph through faith, mentorship, and community support.
- **Men of Promises** – Guiding men back to Christ through accountability, spiritual leadership, and hands-on service.

In 2024, I received a call that reminded me just how far God has brought me.
The Metro Public Health Department created an annual honor in my name:

The Dr. Larry Powell Mental Health Award
Presented for protecting, improving, and sustaining mental health in recognition of your outstanding and profound impact in the community.

That moment humbled me to tears. I thought about the boy who once ran from the law now being recognized for changing lives through faith, advocacy, and service.

From five felonies to a doctoral robe, from prison to preaching, from the trap to transformation, this journey has been nothing short of divine.

I'm not saying I've done everything right. But when it came to my parents, my family, and my purpose, I gave it everything I had. And even when I was broken, God still saw something worth saving.

HONORS & SERVICE

- Delivered the memorial tribute for *Rev. Autura Eason Williams*, a beloved United Methodist Elder whose life was tragically taken by gun violence in 2022.
- Honored by the Metro Public Health Department with the *Dr. Larry Powell Strong Minds, Strong Men Award* for community mental-health advocacy.
- Serves as an Elder at Mount Zion Baptist Church, mentoring men and supporting Saints in Solitude Prison Ministry.
- Helped countless young men graduate from the *4:13 Strong Program*, guiding them toward stability and faith-driven success between the ages of 18 and 30.
- Board and spiritual leader for the *Still Standin Foundation* and *Men of Promises* organizations, where he also received the *Men of Promises Community Service Award.*
- Recognized at halftime during a Nashville soccer game for outstanding community impact and youth mentorship.
- Board member of IDEA (*Indigent Defense and Excellence in Advocacy*), ensuring incarcerated individuals have access to quality legal defense.
- Recipient of the Social Justice Impact Award through the *Mary Catherine Strobel Volunteer Awards*, honoring his ongoing work in advocacy and redemption.

FINAL REFLECTION & CLOSING THOUGHTS

I used to chase validation from the streets.
Now, I chase purpose from God.

Every platform I stand on, every young man I mentor, and every message I preach is a reminder that grace still wins even when the odds don't.

The trap taught me how to survive.
God taught me how to serve.
And now, I'm not just living proof of change
I'm living proof of redemption.

Every scar tells a story, and every loss carved purpose deeper into my life. I've learned that pain doesn't always mean punishment; it often means preparation. What felt like breaking was really God bending me into purpose. I stand today not as a man who escaped the trap, but as one who was transformed in it. My story isn't about survival it's about surrender. Because when I finally let go, God took everything that was broken and made it whole. Pain has become my teacher. It taught me how to pray without pride and how to trust without proof. It reminded me that faith isn't built on what God prevents, it's built on what He preserves.

Even now, I see how every tear had a purpose. I once thought I was losing everything, but really, God was preparing me for where He was taking me.

Rest in Peace Acknowledgments

One of the most tragic realities of *The Trap* is the number of deaths a person witnesses while grinding and surviving within it.

Death wasn't just a story; we heard it, we saw it, we lived through it, and it changed us.

The names below belong to people I personally knew. Some were friends, others were mentors, family, or fellow hustlers just trying to make it out. Whether their time in my life was brief or long, their presence left an imprint. Their stories became lessons, their memories became motivation, and their lives, though cut short, continue to speak through mine.

This section is dedicated to honoring them. May they Rest In Peace:

Lil Granny

Big Sloppy

A. J

Woody

Lil Pete

Robert Brooks

Miss Billie

Uncle George

Floyd Williams

Fat Boy

Uncle Gary aka Uncle G

Jawauntez Powell

Jacquall Powell

Malia Powell

Ty

Ms. Shirley

Larry Thomas Powell (Pops)

8-Hype

www.ingramcontent.com/pod-product-compliance
Lightning Source LLC
LaVergne TN
LVHW090320110126
829402LV00001B/1

* 9 7 9 8 2 1 8 8 3 9 2 6 0 *